THE
NFT
HANDBOOK

*The 2022 Crash Course on How to Create,
Sell and Buy Non-Fungible Tokens with Every
Secret Revealed*

Nathan Real

Table of Contents

INTRODUCTION

NATHAN REAL

Introduction

A non-fungible token (NFT) is a distinct and unit of information that is non-interchangeable recorded on a digital ledger that cannot be exchanged for another ticket (blockchain). NFTs may be connected with digital items that can be reproduced, such as photographs, movies, and audio. In the case of NFTs, a digital ledger is used to offer a publicly accessible authenticity certificate or evidence of ownership. Still, the relation to the data file itself is not restricted from being shared or copied. Because NFTs are not interchangeable (fungible), they differ from blockchain-based cryptocurrencies such as Bitcoin in this respect. When it comes to the energy costs and carbon footprint connected with confirming blockchain transactions, as well as their widespread usage in art frauds, NFTs have come under fire.

Further concerns question the utility of producing evidence of possession in a market that is often uncontrolled and beyond the legal system. It is possible to have confidence in NFT technology since it ensures that nodes will always function no matter what happens to the blockchain. As a result, nothing can indeed happen to the information. The reason for this is not just the quantity of money they earn but also the sums of money they safeguard.

Non-fungible tokens have a variety of advantages, which demonstrates the reasoning for their astronomically considerable appeal. Non-fungible tokens are unquestionably one of the most exciting developments in the world of internet commerce. Furthermore, these benefits have developed into viable selling factors for various consumers. While the benefits of non-fungible tokens create a positive picture of their future, it is crucial to be aware of the restrictions of these tokens. For example, in the case of NFTs, a lack of laws and a standard, universal infrastructure presents several difficulties in their implementation.

Although there are certain limits to NFTs, the positives outweigh them every time. It is feasible to overcome the current boundaries of NFTs by making minor modifications to their design. To overcome the indivisibility of NFTs, for example, fractional ownership may be used in conjunction with other strategies. As non-fungible tokens have applications in a variety of industries, it is critical to consider how they might be used to their benefit in those industries. You may begin studying further about NFTs and discovering strategies to use their blessings to get the most outstanding possible outcomes.

CHAPTER NO. 1
NFT BASICS

NATHAN REAL

Chapter No. 1
NFT Basics

For actual or virtual objects, an NFT — which means for the non-fungible token — acts as a proof of authenticity, similar to a certificate of ownership. Every change in ownership of the digital file is validated by a global network and registered in the public ledger of the blockchain network, which stores the unique digital file. This implies that the proper documentation is permanently noted in the file itself, making it difficult to replace it with a fake. Bitcoins and other cryptocurrencies, on the other hand, are fungible tokens; similar to the United States dollar, every bitcoin is equivalent to any other, while NFTs are just one. Since its inception, the majority of NFT sales have been conducted in digital currencies such as Ether and recorded on the Ethereum blockchain. At the same time, this is not a necessity of the form.

In addition to the electronic piece of art and film clip, the NFT file does not include the Shatner card in its original form. In essence, it's a form of contract that states "the holder of this NFT possesses this other digital file," and it's often accompanied with a hyperlink to the art file itself. Aside from being utilized as unforgeable digitized tickets to events, NFTs might also be used as ownership records for real estate transactions. After all, they are nothing more than one-of-a-kind pieces of code with a verifiably long chain of ownership attached. This concept was first put to use in a video game called CryptoKitties. Since 2017, users have been able to purchase and trade collector NFTs tied to particular virtual cats, with values reaching six figures at the beginning of this year.

Top Shot, a thriving NBA collectible clips firm, is also owned by Dapper Labs, the same company that created Crypto Kitties. Top Shot sold $230 million in NFTs related to basketball highlights from October through January. When it comes to collecting, the attractiveness of NFTs is obvious. Rather than depending on forensics or spotty document records to establish that a work of art or a trading card is legitimate, the authentication is written directly into the NFT file themselves. The attractiveness of the non-fungible tokens (NFTs) that are now being purchased and traded for millions is much less noticeable.

In contrast to an actual trading card, which someone could appreciate for its rarity in a historic production run or seek to complete a collection, an NFT file is not in itself a material trading card. In addition, it is not a work of art, much alone a well-known work of art with an established reputation as a work of elegance or historical significance. Moreover, in the instance of the digital files frequently connected to NFTs, anybody may view the same basketball clips whenever they want or save a copy of the same digital picture with their hard drive. A non-financial transaction (NFT) does nothing more than re-verify and document the provenance of the NFT itself, much like a limited production of a photograph — but when the work of art connected to the NFT is freely available, there is no inherent reason why the NFT should have any value at all. At this point, the collective imaginations of the market come into play. Because they lack intrinsic value, non-financial instruments (NFTs) are analogous to the way that artwork and trading cards may operate as financial products for investors.

Even though the high art market is supported by an economy of specialists and tastemakers who theoretically affect the value of particular art pieces, the elite art market has been disconnected from any tangible reality for many decades.

The majority of art purchasers purchase works of art because they are valuable, not because they are works of art, and then keep them in storage houses until they are ready to liquidate them as an asset on their records and sell them to a new buyer who likewise appreciates them as a financial asset. The trading card market exploded in 2020, with selling prices for rare cards consistently breaking records. For example, a card featuring Michael Jordan and LeBron James sold for $900,000 in February, a different LeBron card sold for $1.8 million in July, and a Giannis Antetokounmpo card sold for $1.81 million in September. A 1909 Honus Wagner baseball card sold for $3.25 million at an auction in October. The cards themselves did not alter, but as an investment market, they were increasingly appealing to traders and investors searching for a haven with prospective rewards, much like fine art. NFTs use the same premise — that anything unique and verifiable may be used as a location to store money and earn returns — and apply it to an imagined real or virtual item, regardless of its physical or virtual form. In an auction on a website devoted only to selling NFTs of tweets, Jack Dorsey, the founder and CEO of Twitter, will auction off an NFT tied to his first tweet, with the highest price now standing at $2.5 million. Some individuals sell non-financial derivatives (NFTs) of other people's artwork without permission. You could try your hand at trading an NFT for the moon if you wanted to.

However, this production of wealth out of thin air comes at an actual financial cost to the economy. Processing Bitcoin transactions necessitates a significant amount of computational power, prompting environmentalists to express alarm about cryptocurrency development. Joanie Lemercier, a French artist, concerned about the environment and regularly monitors the energy use of his studio, was shocked to discover that the sale of only six of his paintings as NFTs consumed more power in one day than he had used in the preceding two years. On a bigger scale, it is believed that the computer networks that comprise the bitcoin and ethereum blockchains use as much power as Argentina and Ecuador each year.

Beyond the high energy costs, there is no assurance that NFTs will maintain any of their value in the long run — just as there was no reason to believe that a bit of paper with a photograph of Honus Wagner on it would ever really be worth more than the cardstock it was published on in 1909 would ever be good enough to justify more than the cardstock it was published on in 1909. However, many musicians are cashed in on the fad for the time being. A piece of art with an NFT on it may bring in thousands of dollars for those trying to make money from their work by seeking tips or selling tangible prints before. The music industry, too, has started to dangle its toes in the waters of virtual reality. Last Friday, kings of Leon released the album through all the usual distribution channels. Still, they also decided to drop three NFTs simultaneously, flavoring the agreement for the fan base (who may also be NFT traders) by offering album bonus payments, live show perks, and additional artwork to those who purchased NFTs at the time of release.

1.1 What Is NFT?

Digital assets that symbolize various things such as collectibles, artwork, and other in-game goods are known as non-fungible tokens. Non-fungible tokens (NFTs) are often exchanged online with most cryptocurrency transactions and are encoded inside a smart contract running on a blockchain. Non-Fungible Tokens (NFTs) turn numerous electronic artworks and collectibles into traceable and one-of-a-kind assets that can be exchanged simply on the blockchain. To better understand the notion, it is necessary first to grasp what the terms 'fungible' and 'non-fungible' refer to.

If anything is non-fungible, it signifies that it is one-of-a-kind and cannot be replaced by anything else.

The fact that you have an original trading card and swap it for another means that you will end up with something unique. Rare coins, limited-edition Jordan stuffs, and even Pokémon cards come to mind as examples of high-value collectibles. Non-fungible objects have one-of-a-kind characteristics, which implies that even if several copies of the item were made, there'd always be only one unique item in existence. Certification of authenticity is included with non-fungible tokens, which creates scarcity among accessible assets. Tweets, video games skins, GIFs, virtual trade cards, and digital real estate are just a few examples of non-fungible tokens (NFTs). Unlike cash, Bitcoin and other cryptocurrencies, on the other hand, may be exchanged for any other cryptocurrency. Trading one bitcoin for another will result in the acquisition of the same amount of currency. As an additional illustration, consider the following scenario: you have a $100 note; you may exchange it for two $50 bills, and the worth will be the same.

Even though the NFT market is now buzzing with virtual Mona Lissa, the issue remains what other forms of NFTs are out there in the wild besides tweets and images. Let's take a plunge into the realm of NFTs and see if we can discover a solution to this question.

However, try constructing an exact reproduction of the Mona Lisa, up to the brushwork and the actual paper, instead of digital material, which can be simply copied and circulated. Consider NFTs to be digital works of art that are not reproducible. These are attributes that can't be duplicated or changed in any way, shape, or form.

Indeed, the material may be duplicated and shared on social media platforms, but the buyer will retain possession of the NFT regardless of what happens. The act of pressing Ctrl + C on an NFT and uploading it is analogous to taking a photograph of a work of art and displaying it on your wall while the original is still in possession of the owner.

1.2 Understanding NFT

Bitcoin and other cryptocurrencies, like actual money, are fungible, which means that they may be traded or swapped for one another. For example, one Bitcoin's value is always the same as the value of another Bitcoin. In the same vein, one unit of Ether is always equivalent to another branch of Ether. Because of their fungibility, cryptocurrencies are well-suited for use as a safe means of exchange in the digital economy, where they have gained widespread acceptance.

Due to the fact that each token is unique and irreplaceable, NFTs alter the cryptographic paradigm, making it almost impossible for a non-fungible token to be considered the same as another. They are digitalized representations of assets that have been compared to digital passports because each token contains a distinctive, non-transferable identity that allows it to be distinguished from the other tokens in circulation. They are also extendable, which means that you may combine two NFTs to create a third, one-of-a-kind NFT by breeding them together. NFTs, like Bitcoin, have ownership information that allows token holders to be easily identified and transferred between one another.

In addition, NFTs enable asset owners to provide information or qualities relevant to the item. For example, in the case of coffee beans, tokens depicting the beans might be recognized as fair trade. Alternatively, artists may sign their electronic artwork by including their signature in the information associated with it. NFTs were developed as a result of the ERC-721 standard. ERC-721 is an intelligent contract system set by some individuals willing to take responsibility for the ERC-20 intellectual contract standard. It defines the bare minimum interface – including security ownership details and metadata –required to exchange and dispersion gaming tokens.

Taking the concept, a step further, the ERC-1155 standard lowers the storage costs and transactions associated with non-fungible tokens while batching numerous non-tokens into one single deal. Cryptokitties, maybe the most well-known use of NFTs, is a good example. Cryptokitties, introduced in November 2017 and had unique identification numbers on the Ethereum blockchain, are digital representations of cats. Each kitty is one-of-a-kind and has a corresponding ether value. They reproduce amongst themselves and generate new offspring, each of whom has unique characteristics and importance compared to their parents. Following their launch, cryptokitties quickly gained a large following, with fans spending more than $20 million in ether to purchase, feed, and otherwise care for them in just a few short weeks.

Some enthusiasts went so far as to spend over $100,000 on the project. Whereas the cryptokitties use scenario may appear inconsequential, the ones that follow it have far-reaching business ramifications. For example, non-fungible tokens (NFTs) have been used in private equity and real estate transactions. Incorporating multiple types of tokens into a single contract has several implications, one of which is the ability to serve as an escrow to various kinds of NFTs, ranging from art to real estate, in a single financial transaction.

1.3 Creating and Buying NFT

NFTs are used to ensure that a unique object — generally a visual image such as a work of art, a musical creation, or an item inside a video game — remains in possession of the owner. Bitcoin (CRYPTO: BTC) and other cryptocurrencies are produced and maintained on a blockchain, the same digital ledger technological system used by these tokens and different kinds of cryptocurrencies. NFTs are mostly built on the Ethereum (CRYPTO: ETH) network, but there are also other blockchains that some NFTs make use of as well, like Solana (CRYPTO: SOL) and Polkadot (CRYPTO: POLD) and others (CRYPTO: DOT). If you think about it, these digital tokens are analogous to a virtual certification or title that you would submit to verify that you possess a tangible asset like real estate. They're a digital proof of ownership initially intended for digital content and artwork.

However, non-financial trusts (NFTs) may also be used to ensure ownership of one-of-a-kind physical assets, which can include everything from real estate to collectibles to real works of art. Unless otherwise noted, we will refer to NFTs as essentially representing virtual assets for this book.

Buying NFT

Non-fungible tokens (NFTs) are purchased and sold via a dedicated NFT marketplace, similar to Amazon (NASDAQ: AMZN) or Etsy (NASDAQ: ETSY), but only for digital assets. These markets may be used to purchase an NFT at a predetermined price or to conduct a virtual auction, similar to the exchange system used to buy and sell cryptocurrencies and equities. As a result, the prices of NFTs posted for sale through auction are volatile, fluctuating in value based on demand. The demand for a product increase as a result of the cost. A significant distinction between NFTs and shares and cryptocurrencies is that stocks and cryptocurrencies are fungible, which means that one unit is identical to the other.

One share of Amazon is just the same as another part of Amazon, and a single Bitcoin token is the same as another Bitcoin token, and so on. As a non-fungible token (NFT), you are purchasing a unique item that any other similar thing cannot replace in the market. It is necessary to establish and fund a bitcoin or crypto bag on an NFT marketplace before you may bid on these digital assets. Like a virtual wallet on an e-commerce site, a crypto wallet keeps the cryptocurrency required to purchase an NFT. A wallet must be filled with the necessary cryptocurrency to buy the desired NFT. For example, an NFT based on the Ethereum blockchain tech may need the purchase of Ether tokens in order to be used in the transaction. The purchasing of NFT is possible via a number of different platforms. OpenSea, Rarible, super rare, and Foundation are some of the most popular NFT markets.

Additionally, various specialist markets specialize in particular assets. To provide an example, NBA Top Shot, which the National Basketball Association controls, offers NFTs in the form of clips of players performing on the court. Irrespective of the market, a cryptocurrency wallet will need to be created and paid before bidding on and purchasing an NFT is possible.

How to Purchase an NFT?

The vast majority of NFT operations take place in a specialized marketplace. Here's a brief walkthrough of the process of purchasing these digital items from there. Currently, most markets rely on the Ethereum program to facilitate their transactions. As a result, in order to buy an NFT, you will require Ethereum's native coin, Ether. It is possible to register an account with an alternative like Binance or WazirX and purchase the tokens if you do not already have one.

In addition, you must create a cryptocurrency wallet that is compatible with Ethereum. A cryptocurrency wallet is a digitalized location where you may keep your coins safe and secure. You may open wallets with cryptocurrency exchanges such as Metamask, Binance, and Coindesk. To create a wallet with a platform of your choice, you must first visit the website of the system of your choice and register. Following the creation of the wallet, you will be required to transfer the ether you purchased from the exchanges to the wallet's address.

Select the marketplace from which you want to purchase the NFT. NFTs may be found in a variety of different markets, and Rarible, OpenSea, and Foundation are just a few of the best non-traditional trading platforms.

Create an account on the online marketplace of your choice. Various markets have a variety of different registration procedures.

Connecting your account to the marketplace is simple. The majority of markets include a straightforward 'Connect wallet' feature on their platforms.

Look through the market and choose an NFT that appeals to you. In order to purchase NFTs, most markets have an auction mechanism in place; you will need to place a bid for the NFT you desire.

When you place a winning offer, you will finish the transactions, and the appropriate cash will be deducted from your wallet as soon as possible. Keep in mind that you may also be required to pay a transaction charge to the marketplace. However, the amount of the cost will vary depending on the market.

Selling NFT

Once you have purchased an NFT, you have complete control over the digital asset and may use it in any way you see fit. You may retain it as a collection, put it on display for others to see, or utilize it as a component of a more considerable digital undertaking. You may also put it up for sale on your website. Marketplaces impose a fee for non-cash transactions. Because the blockchain processing required to validate the NFT requires energy, these fees might change depending on which blockchain system the NFT is using. This is referred to as a "gas charge." The piece of the digital asset you hold will need to be published to the marketplace of your choosing, which will only work if your chosen market supports the blockchain upon which the NFT was developed. From there, you can decide whether to post it for sale at a fixed price or whether to have auction-style sales in which purchasers submit bids on the item.

Once the item has been submitted, it will be verified by the marketplace. Following the sale, the marketplace will take care of transferring NFT from seller to buyer as well as transferring crypto money into your wallet minus the listing charge and any associated blockchain computing fees (if any).

Creating NFT

Part of the appeal of NFTs comes from content creators — artists, singers, filmmakers, authors, and others — who can ensure the integrity of their work while also monetizing it via the use of NFTs to generate income. An NFT may be created by anybody (or "minted") and sold on a cryptocurrency exchange or other marketplace.

The minting procedure varies somewhat according to the platform, but the essential steps are as follows:

• Make sure you have a cryptocurrency wallet set up and charged

• Click on the "create" option and upload your artwork within the marketplace.

1.4 Investment in NFT

The NFT movement is very young, and it serves as an early indication of the potential that cryptocurrencies have to make digitalization more accessible to a broader range of individuals. For artists, the creation and sale of digital assets may make a lot of financial sense. However, when purchasing NFTs for their monetary worth as a collectible, they are considered a speculative purchase. The value of the work is inherently unknown and will change in response to the desire for the product itself. There is no hard and fast rule for determining which collectibles will grow and decline in value—detecting a new NFT pattern early on, on the other hand, can be pretty helpful in the long run. The value of specific digital works of art once sold for pennies on the dollar has increased to several thousand dollars. If you have a keen eye for music, art, and other forms of collectibles, and you love doing so, becoming involved in non-traditional investing may be a good idea.

When purchasing an asset, some factors to look for include the originator of the investment, how unique the item is, the history of the asset's ownership, and whether or not the support can be utilized to create money after it has been acquired (for example, payment to view a piece or relicensing fees). In response to the claim that NFTs are a "bubble" ready to burst, it should be noted that bubbles are frequently only discovered after the fact.

However, keep in mind that this does not alter the reality that digital assets may, at some time in the future, experience a downturn in value. Calculate and diversify the risks associated with your investments — for example, by including cryptocurrencies in your NFT portfolio as well as stocks of companies developing blockchain technology. NFTs are still in their infancy as a research and development tool. Even if it's a potential new front in the technology world, there are dangers associated with investing in a movement in its infancy. Maintain caution as you gain more knowledge about non-financial-transactions (NFTs). Remember to keep your assets diversified to reduce the chance of any investment trying to derail your wealth-building efforts.

Is It Worthwhile to Invest in NFT?

Aimed for the high-risk investor, NFTs provide an extraordinarily unique and potentially lucrative chance to generate significant profits—but be cautioned, this is very rare and only occurs in exceptional circumstances. If you're searching for a more reliable method to invest your money, rather than a GIF of a Pop-Tart cat, think about investing in an index fund, which is less glamorous and does not have the same cultural cache as a Pop-Tart cat GIF.

In order to join the realm of non-fungible tokens, though, you'll need first to create a digital wallet in your computer's browser.

This is where you'll keep your cryptocurrencies and non-fungible tokens (NFTs). Afterward, you'll need to seek NFTs on platforms like OpenSea.io or Rarible, select the one you want, then acquire the appropriate cryptocurrency for that specific NFT before making your purchase.

After then, it's just a waiting game. Because the value of your NFT is determined by how much someone else is prepared to pay for it, both you and your Pop-Tart cat are at the mercy of the marketplace at any one time.

1.5 Difference Between NFT and Cryptocurrency

NFT is short for Non-Fungible Token. It's often developed using the same sort of software design as cryptocurrencies, like Ethereum and Bitcoin, but that's is where the similarities stop. Physical cash and cryptocurrency are "fungible," which may be traded or swapped for one another. They're also equally valuable dollar has always been worth another dollar; a single Bitcoin is always equivalent to another Bitcoin. Crypto's fungibility makes it a reliable way of completing blocks of transactions. NFTs are distinct. Each contains a digital certificate that makes it nearly impossible for NFTs to be swapped for or equivalent to one another (hence, non-fungible). One NBA Top Shot clip, for instance, is not equal to every day merely because they're both NFTs. (One NBA Top Shot footage isn't necessarily equivalent to some other NBA Top Shot clip, for that matter.)

1.6 How Auction Works at Marketplace?

Auction marketplace is a multi-side platform that links sellers and buyers, where vendors bid or contest for the goods or service. The distinction from the stock market is that the seller rather than the fixed price sets a low bid. Buyers begin to bid as much as they desire. After that, the item goes to the bidder with the highest offer. The crucial aspect is that this procedure is entirely transparent and open to sellers and buyers. There are three primary sorts of the auction you may provide on your platform:

Increment Auction

The increment is a rise of an amount over a specified number. In bidding, increments are a minimum level an auction offer must be increased each time the current highest bid is exceeded. For example, have a glance at the bid increments table on eBay. If the current price of the goods is $1.00-$4.99, the following offer must be at least $0.25 higher. For example, you offer a product, the beginning price would be $20, and the incremental bid is $10. If someone enters a bid of $50, it will be instantly boosted by $10. After this, no one may submit an offer less than $60.

Reserve Price Auction

A Reserve price auction enables the buyer to specify a lower price they want to sell for. Usually, this price is disguised, so the purchasers may only see whether or not it has been satisfied. When the limit price is reached, the highest offer wins the auction. For example, you sell a piece of antique jewelry and set a guide price of $40, with a beginning price of $2. In this example, individuals may start bidding at $2, but if until the conclusion of the auction the bidding hasn't reached $40, your jewelry will not be auctioned.

Automatic auction

An automated auction is the simplest method to bid. In this situation, buyers specify the most excellent price they wish to pay for the product and bid autonomously on the buyer's behalf. If another bidder submits the higher cost, the prior buyer will be overbid, and their request will terminate.

1.7 Case Study

Paris Hilton. Mark Cuban. Steph Curry Eminem. The whole list of celebs who have adopted non-fungible tokens – whether by producing, collecting, or advertising – seems to get more prominent by the minute, and it spans the range from Lil Nas X to Rob Gronkowski. NFTs are here. They're no longer bordering. Precisely, collectible and art NFTs have gone popular with fantastic speed — quicker than even the most starry-eyed, the to-the-moon crypto bull could have dreamt. We now have a more precise grasp of why. As stated earlier, NFTs (particularly art and collectibles) are enjoyable, visualizable, culturally significant, and they're simple to grasp in a manner that many blockchain ideas are not. They can address real-world challenges.

Then there's the growth that many in the field – myself included – badly underestimated: the community aspect. The social aspect. When you pay for a Bored Ape Yacht Club, World of Women NFT, or cryptopunk, it indicates that you got it and participate in the club. "People relate with them on a human level," said Maria Shen, a director at Electric Capital, a blockchain-focused venture capital (VC) company. "Ownership reveals something essential about their identity; it speaks something about their desires." This we now comprehend. But what's next?

Only a year ago, art and collectible NFTs were essentially concepts with "potentials," but no one outside of the crypto community took them seriously. What categories now are in that similar period of early conjecture, which will erupt? What will goofy-sounding NFT be sponsored by Tom Brady in 2022? What innovative, industry-disrupting NFT would Ariana Grande advocate in 2023? What are the future chapters of this extraordinary narrative? Discussion with a brain trust of NFT insiders — investors, entrepreneurs, individuals who thrive non-fungible tokens – offers us a view into the (potential) future. Some of these groups will appear apparent, and some will appear far-fetched. Some could even seem ludicrous. Yet examined, they can revolutionize how we consume material, how we spend and generate money, how we verify our identity, how we attend an event, how we behave, or even how or where we spend the majority of our time.

According to the company, the small blobs of Axie Infinity are played by 2 million individuals every day, currently valued at 3 billion dollars. According to Devin Finzer, Chief executive Officer of OpenSea, the world's largest NFT platform, "Gaming is exhilarating because you already have millions of people who are purchasing digitalized goods inside of games." Finzer believes that the reason we haven't seen more widespread adoption yet is that "the development cycle with games is a little longer than with collectible projects and simpler arts," he explained. A bit extra time has been added to the wait." He anticipates that the results of these improvements will be seen within a single year or two.

Jamie Burke, Chief Executive officer of Outlier Ventures (a blockchain venture capital and accelerator lab based in the United Kingdom), was initially inspired by research showing that "people spend five times more time playing a blockchain game than they do playing a conventional game." He said that at first, doubters "poo-pooed" this study, but then Axie entered the picture. In Burke's opinion, the Axie juggernaut serves as proof that a gamer is given the option to exit the game by cashing out in cryptocurrency and is given complete freedom to "do whatever they damn well please with the cash" they will spend more money. As a result, he predicts that Axie is only the start of a much larger gaming boom that will be "huge in the next decade" and that it will be "huge in the next decade."

"The luxury brands are entering the NFT area," adds Laglasse smoking a cigarette during our Zoom conference call. On September 30, the famous brand Dolce and Gabbana sold its first nine-piece selection of NFTs, dubbed "Collezione Genesi," a surreal combination of high fashion and blockchain technology, for a great value of $5.6 million, making it the most expensive NFT collection ever sold. The collection comprised tangible objects (such as women's clothes) and their digital counterparts, NFTs. A fresh brand called Auroboros, which explains itself as "the very first fashion house to merge technology and science with physical couture," debuted a line of virtual apparel that you can "wear" using augmented reality just two weeks earlier, during London Fashion Week (AR). To put things in perspective, this did not occur during a crypto-related conference, and this happened during the London Fashion Week.

Should You Buy NFTs?

Just since you can purchase NFTs, does it imply you should? It varies. NFTs are dangerous since their future is unpredictable, and we don't yet have a lot of experience to gauge their performance. Since NFTs are so new, it may be worth the modest investment sums to check it out for now. In other words, investment in NFTs is a mainly personal choice. If you have extra cash to spend, it may be essential to consider, particularly if a work bears importance.

But bear in mind, an NFT's value is entirely predicated on what someone else is prepared to pay for it. Consequently, desire will drive the price instead of technical, fundamental, or financial conditions, which often impact stock prices and approximately constitute the Foundation for investor demand.

All this implies, an NFT may resell for less than you bought for it. Or you may not be able to resale it at all if nobody wants it.

NFTs are also subjected to taxes on capital gains when you sell equities at a profit. Since they're regarded collectibles, however, they may not enjoy the good long-term capital gains rates stocks do and may potentially be taxed at a greater collectibles tax rate, though the IRS has not yet established what NFTs are deemed for tax reasons. Bear in mind, the cryptocurrencies used to acquire the NFT may also be taxed if they've gained in value since you purchased them, so you may want to check in with a tax specialist when contemplating adding NFTs to your portfolio.

That said, treat NFTs just as you would any investment: Do your homework, know the risks that you may lose all of your investment dollars—and if you decide to leap, go with a healthy dosage of caution.

CHAPTER NO. 2
HISTORY OF NFTS

NATHAN REAL

Chapter No. 2
History of NFTs

Here is the history of non-fungible tokens:

2.1 The First Five Years of History

(2014–2017)

The presentation of Etheria took place on November 13, 2015, at DEVCON 1. Quantum, the first known "NFT," was constructed by Anil Dash and Kevin McCoy in May 2014 and consisted of a video clip created by McCoy's wife Jennifer and other components. During a live broadcast for the Seven-on-Seven summit meeting in New York City at the New Museum, McCoy published the footage on the Namecoin blockchain and auctioned it to Dash for $4 on the Namecoin network. As McCoy and Dash put it, the technique was referred to as "monetized graphics." Through the use of on-chain information, a non-fungible that is a marketable blockchains marker was expressly tied to a one-of-a-kind piece of art (enabled by Namecoin).

This is different from the cross-unit, fungible, metadata-less called "colored coins" of many other blockchains, including Counterparty, which are not fungible and do not include metadata.

After three months the creation of the blockchain Ethereum, the very first NFT initiative, Etheria, was announced and exhibited at DEVCON 1, Ethereum's inaugural developer conference, which took place in London, United Kingdom, in October of 2015. After being unsold for more than five years, the majority of Etheria's 457 marketable and traded hexagonal tiles were finally snapped up on March 13, 2021, when revived interest in NFTs ignited a purchasing frenzy. For a total of $1.4 million, all tiles from the current and previous versions, each of which was hardcoded at 1 ETH ($0.43 at the time of the release), were sold in less than 24 hours. It was only with the introduction of the ERC-721 standard, originally suggested on the Ethereum GitHub in 2017 and followed by the launch of a number of NFT initiatives that year, that the word "NFT" received widespread acceptance. The Curio Cards project, CryptoPunks (a venture to trade unique cartoon characters, created by the American company Larva Labs on the Ethereum blockchain), and the Decentraland platform are just a few examples. All three initiatives were mentioned in the initial proposal, and a set of rare Pepe trading cards were included.

2.2 Late 2017–2021

(Awareness among the wider populace)

The popularity of CryptoKitties, an online video game in which participants adopt and exchange virtual kittens, sparked public interest in non-financial tokens. Soon after its introduction, the idea went viral, generating $12.5 million worth of investment and resulting in the sale of particular kittens for more than $100,000 apiece.

The popularity of CryptoKitties led to the addition of CryptoKitties to the ERC-721 standards, which was formed in January 2018 (and completed in June). It confirmed the usage of the phrase "non-fungible token" to relate to "non-fungible tokens." In 2018, Decentraland, a blockchain-based virtual space that launched its token sales in August 2017 and had a $20 million domestic market as of September 2018, raised $26 million in an initial coin offering and had a total market capitalization of $26 million. Following the success of CryptoKitties, another comparable NFT-based online game, Axie Infinity, was created in March 2018 and went on to become the world's most valuable NFT collection in May 2021, after which it was discontinued. In 2019, Nike received a patent for a system known as CryptoKicks, which would employ NFTs to validate the authenticity of actual shoes and provide the consumer with a virtual replica of the shoe in exchange for their payment.

During the first quarter of 2020, Dapper Labs, the company that created CryptoKitties, unveiled the beta version of NBA TopShot, a program that would offer tokenized memorabilia of NBA highlights. The project was completed on top of the Flow blockchain, which is a younger and much more efficient blockchain when compared to the Ethereum blockchain. Later the same year, the initiative was made available to the general public, and as of February 28, 2021, it has generated over $230 million in gross revenues. During 2020, the NFT market enjoyed fast expansion, with its total value doubling to $250 million. NFTs accounted for more than $200 million in spending during the first two to three months of 2021.

2.3 From 2021 to the Present

(Increased demand for NFTs)

Following a series of high-profile transactions, interest in nonferrous metals (NFTs) rose in the first few months of 2021. Digital art made by the band Grimes, an NFT of the Nyan Cat meme, and NFTs designed by 3LAU to advertise his album Ultraviolet were among the NFTs sold in February 2021. A number of highly publicized NFT sales occurred in March 2021, including an NFT designed to encourage the Kings of Leon soundtrack 'When

You See Yourself,' a $69.3 million sale of vector graphics by Mike Winkelmann entitled 'Every day: The First 5000 Days,' and an NFT created by Twitter founder Jack Dorsey that depicted his very first tweet. Because of the speculative nature of the NFT market, more investors are trading at higher volumes and rates.

Experts have referred to the recent spike in NFT purchases as an economic bubble and have likened it to the Dot-com boom. By the middle of April 2021, demand looked to have significantly waned, resulting in a dramatic drop in prices; early purchasers were said to have "done extraordinarily well" by the publication Bloomberg Businessweek. An NFT of the source code for the World Wide Web, ascribed to internet creator scientist of a computer named Sir Tim Berners-Lee, was sold by Sotheby's in London in June 2021, and the proceeds were donated to the Internet Archive. And was sold for a total of US$5.4 million. According to the auction house, Sotheby's acquired a package of 101 Bored Ape Yacht Club NFTs for $24.4 million in September 2021.

CHAPTER NO. 3
TYPES OF NFT

NATHAN REAL

Chapter No. 3
Types Of NFT

The concept of what constitutes an NFT is still somewhat ambiguous, with the result that fundamentally anything may be categorized as an NFT. Here is a list of the most prevalent and reasonable NFTs currently available on the market.

3.1 Art

In the current era, art NFTs are among the most prevalent forms of NFTs. Consider a group of Apes who are bored and a group of Punks who are bored. Digital art enthusiasts are not unique from those who like real art. Status, beauty, the social component, and patronage are just a few things that NFT enthusiasts look for in such works of art.

Record companies, marketing outlets, and streaming services have been criticized for being unfair to musicians, with the vast majority of the money going to them rather than the artists. Music non-fungible tokens (NFT) initiatives such as Sound, Arpeggi Labs, and Royal are already sprouting up, enabling musicians to have more control over their work. Music NFTs provide artists the opportunity to produce a collectible and listeners the chance to become part of a limited group of superfans.

The most often practiced type of NFT is an artistic expression. The creation of NFTs provided an excellent chance for designers to sell their greatest works online in the same way they would sell them in a physical store. At the moment, many of the costliest non-linear optical transducers are pieces of art. "EVERYDAY'S: THE FIRST 5000 DAYS," by famous artist Beeple, is the most value NFT ever sold, according to Luno, making it the most expensive NFT ever sold. An incredible $69 million was paid for this painting. There are additionally very costly non-financial transactions (NFTs) that are destroying the financial accounts of billionaires.

This holds for pieces of video art as well. Short films and even animated GIFs have been selling fast for millions of dollars. Notably, a repeating 10-second film called "Crossroad," which depicts a nude Donald Trump sprawled on the ground went for $6.6 million and was the most expensive video ever sold on eBay. This one was created by Beeple as well.

3.2 Access

These digital tokens enable broadly interoperable and low-friction access while maintaining high security. This kind of NFT may be utilized to give electronic access to video classes or a personal discord server, among other things.

3.3 Objects in a Game

When it comes to gaming, virtual products are commonplace, with Web 2.0 players spending about $40 billion annually on virtual goods. On the other hand, these virtual items stay the corporation's property rather than being transferred to the gamers. Another unfortunate aspect is that these items are not interoperable with one another. Game NFTs from games, such as Axie Infinity, allow the user to acquire NFTs predicated on their accomplishments while playing the game itself.

3.4 Music

Music is also a prominent component of the NFT spectrum. Music has been a fungible product for decades, having been produced and delivered on various media, including records, CDs, cassettes, and now digitally over the internet. NFTs, on the other hand, have become more popular with artists and DJs, resulting in some of them earning millions of dollars in a matter of a few hours.

Because of cutbacks made by streaming platforms and record labels, musicians often only get a percentage of the revenue generated by their work. When it comes to non-financial transactions, artists may retain around 100 percent of the money, which is why many music artists are turning this way.

3.5 Redeemable

They depict a model in which a digitalized token can be redeemed for tangible goods. High-end collectors use vaults to store their collections, a perfect example. In order to reduce the number of intermediaries and friction, redeemable NFTs are digital presentations of such compilations that can be traded and showcased digitally.

3.6 Video-Game-Related Items

With video games, we have reached another frontier in the NFT domain. Companies are not selling whole games as non-transferable tokens. Instead, they'll sell in-game material such as characters, skins, and other accessories. At the moment, users may purchase dozens of records of DLC assets. An NFT item, on the other hand, will be unique and exclusive to a single customer. NFT allows developers to sell ordinary DLC while also selling a particular DLC version on the NFT marketplace.

3.7 Memes

If you were under the impression that the World Wide Web couldn't get any more entertaining, the NFT market now allows you to buy and sell memes. A unique feature is that in certain circumstances, the person shown in the meme is the person who is selling the item. Several of the most well-known memes, including disaster girl, Nyan Cat, Bad Luck Brian, and others, appear on the list, with earnings ranging from $30,000 to $770,000 per meme. The Doge meme, the most precious meme to date, was sold for a whopping $4 million at a recent auction.

3.8 Identity

There have been numerous instances of compromised personal information throughout the web two eras. Better methods of identifying yourself are being promoted, such as the Sign in With Ethereum feature. Identity management systems such as ENS simplify sharing data across multiple platforms. When it comes to revealing things like qualifications, reputation, and records selectively, NFTs will make it simple.

3.9 Databases on the Web 2.0

People may use decentralized data stores and cryptographic techniques to extend NFTs to any data kept in a centralized Web 2.0 database via decentralized data stores and cryptographic methods. Consider your complete social network or even you're watching interests, as one example. With the help of these NFTs, you may easily transition from one reality to another.

3.10 Trading Cards and Other Collectibles

NFTs may be compared to digital trading cards in several ways. It is common knowledge that special edition baseball cards can sell for millions of dollars, and the NFT industry is no exception. It is possible to exchange and purchase computer-generated copies of trading cards on the market, and they may be kept in the same way that genuine trading cards are supported. And, much like the actual thing, some of these replicas fetch more than a million dollars in price. It is possible for businesses to sell various sorts of collecting items, not simply trading cards, on the NFT market. If anything is considered collectible, it can be placed up for sale on the open market.

3.11 Bringing Everything to a Close

Anyone may categorize and sell their goods, as shown by creating an NFT of the very first tweet by Twitter's inventor, Jack Dorsey, in 2011. With so much interest being generated in the NFT environment, concerns such as "Are NFTs in a Bubble?" are likely to arise. What is the monetary value of NFTs? These are complicated issues to answer, but as long as individuals explore the many possibilities, the NFT universe will continue to expand.

3.12 Sports

NFTs provide something that cannot be replicated in the physical world: a recollection of unforgettable sporting occasions. These are brief videos of historical events in sports, such as game-changing slam dunks or game-changing touchdowns that are worth seeing. Despite the fact that these recordings may be as brief as 10 seconds in length, they can fetch upwards of $200,000.

3.13 Domain Names

NFT fever has expanded to domain names, which are not immune to the disease. It is possible to register a domain name and then sell it on the NFT market, and this has several advantages over other options. You will often be required to pay an outside party business to administer your domain name. If you purchase one on the NFT marketplace, you will be eligible to claim sole ownership of the word, therefore eliminating the need for a third-party intermediary.

3.14 Virtual Fashion

Everything purchased and traded on the NFT market has been done virtually, so why should style be distinct? Virtual Fashion You may spend a lot of money on a fantastic costume, but you won't be able to wear it properly. Instead of dressing up their real-life avatars, those who purchase Fashion NFTs will do it online.

This may seem absurd, but keep in mind that someone paid $4 million to acquire the Doge meme somewhere in this world. Being the proud owner of a virtual purse or jewelry is reserved for the more lavish and fashion-forward. These, of course, will all be one-of-a-kind creations with a limited number available.

3.15 Miscellaneous Items

The other elements on this list were straightforward to describe, but the NFT market is somewhat of a wild west of online business, as seen by the NFT market meltdown that occurred a few months ago. As previously indicated, Jack Dorsey essentially sold a single tweet. This opens the door for anyone to sell whatever they want on the NFT market, which is indeed what it is for. Whether it is tweets, articles, Facebook statuses, Snapchat Stories or TikToks, the sky is the limit to what people may sell on the internet.

Much potential exists in the NFT sector that has yet to be explored. People have bought a wide variety of items as NFTs, ranging from digitalized baseball postcards to virtual Versace bags, and we are just at the beginning of the iceberg.

CHAPTER NO. 4
BENEFITS OF NFT

NATHAN REAL

Chapter No. 4
Benefits of NFT

Non-fungible Tokens (NFTs) are the current buzzword in the blockchain business, and they are a kind of cryptocurrency. Their emergence as a thrilling subset of the cryptocurrency world has been hailed as a boon. However, with all of the commotion around them, you may be wondering whether or not they are really useful. As a vendor, a buyer, or a potential investment in the future. Consider the following examples of how NFTs will operate to your benefit.

4.1 Decentralized Marketplace

NFTs provide artists the opportunity to profit immediately from their work. An excellent example is the art world, where someone would want the services of an agent in order to sell and advertise their work. These middlemen are eliminated, allowing the artists or the genuine producers to engage and trade directly with their clients via NFTs. This concept also provides additional advantages to the developers by letting them receive a fee for each moment the NFT is traded.

4.2 One-of-a-kind

They are uncommon in the sense that only one of them may exist and that they are challenging to make. In contrast to thousands of NFTs, most artists and sellers will only have a few NFTs in their collection. As a result, it is reasonable to suppose that you will become one of the few persons who will be in possession of these collectibles.

4.3 Collectibles and Memorabilia

In a technical sense, all NFTs have collected items. As previously said, they are one-of-a-kind, and only one of each may be found.

Following the purchase, you have the option to keep them and watch their value grow over time.

4.4 Ability to Resell

The majority of individuals will engage with NFTs because they believe they will profit from them. There are a large number of persons who make a livelihood by reselling these items. Investing in nonferrous metals for their sale price has the potential to provide enormous rewards. Some of these antiques have been resold for more than 20,000 USD when the original buyer spent a few thousand dollars. They earned almost 15,000 USD in only one deal by reselling the items!

4.5 Unchangeable

No one will ever change the information stored on the token. Besides that, it cannot be deleted, lost, or otherwise deleted from the blockchain network. In essence, they are supposed to persist indefinitely since their information will always stay in its original form. This, in and of itself, contributes to their collectability and high monetary worth.

4.6 Copyright Protection by Law

One of the most significant benefits of the NFT technology is that it enables artists and content providers to own the intellectual property completely. Most license agreements do not include language like this, which permits them to continue making cash without relinquishing their copyright rights.

4.7 Security

When it concerns NFTs, you can be confident that your information is safe. Blockchains are decentralized, which means that the data they contain is stored in a number of distinct nodes located worldwide. The database records are

always identical at each node, regardless of which one is used. Even if the internet connection is down, there will always be a record of what happened someplace in the system.

4.8 Authenticity and Ownership

An NFT is, at its heart, a mechanism that uses blockchain technology to produce non-fungible digital assets. Two key advantages may be derived from using these qualities. The certificate of ownership is the primary service provided by NFT. In the case of blockchain-based NFT, the evidence of ownership is safeguarded against alteration or alteration. A digital asset may only have one authorized ownership at a time as a result of this. As a result, customers no longer have to be concerned about the possibility of counterfeiting. Then there's the issue of genuineness. Through the use of NFT, digital items are transformed into non-fungible assets that are associated with unique records. Keeping the assets' worth and entitlement to their owner is possible by maintaining their outstanding records. Furthermore, the immutable blockchain protects NFTs from being altered, removed, or replaced, enabling NFTs to represent authenticity as a desirable feature that they may be traded for.

4.9 Transferability

The trading of NFTs is conducted via the use of smart contracts. A platform is self-contained, secure, accurate, and devoid of interruptions in its operation. It is easier to transfer ownership of NFT when using a smart contract since it just needs the fulfillment of particular requirements between the buyer and seller in accordance with the contract's design.

4.10 Royalties

NFT gives the ability for content providers to maintain complete control of their intellectual property rights. In order to facilitate the creation of smart contracts, NFT encourages content authors to grant ownership of just the content when producing new NFT. Using this arrangement, the unknown content creator will be compensated when their work is sold, and they will also get a royalty payment for each time the new owners sell their content.

4.11 Economic Prospect

Until recently, the primary emphasis of NFT professionals has been on their essential characteristics. Non-linear optical fibers (NFTs) have found widespread use in the field of digital content in recent years. The fragmented character of the digital content market is the crucial reason for the practicality of NFTs in the realm of digital content production.

Content creators and providers are continually challenged with the terror that competing podiums are mining their revenue and decreasing their grossing chances. For instance, a digital artist who publishes their output on social media networks might also generate revenue for the platform by selling advertisements to the artist's admirers. While the artist receives an excellent way to promote, it does not assist the artist in earning any money as a result of the platform's advantages.

The advantages of non-fungible tokens may pave the way for the formation and expansion of a whole new creator economy in the future. The creator's economy would be focused on assisting content producers in avoiding the need to transfer ownership to platforms that they utilize for the purpose of marketing their material.

Thanks to non-financial technologies, the ownership of the material is incorporated only within the content. As a result, when the content producers sell their work, the revenues flow straight to them. If the NFT is sold to a new owner, the creator of the NFT may be able to collect royalties by implementing innovative agreements while developing new NFTs. As long as the NFT metadata contains the inventor's address, the original creator may be eligible to collect royalties from each resale of the token.

4.12 Increase the Rate of Inclusive Growth

The third and most significant point to mention among the benefits of NFTs is their ability to promote equitable growth and development. NFTs connect content producers from different areas into one environment, allowing new paths for inclusive development for all participants. First and foremost, NFT artists may realize the entire worth of their work and engage in direct communication with their target audiences. On the other hand, Buyers have the option of obtaining liquidity in a variety of various kinds of assets via the use of NFTs. For example, the usage of non-financial instruments (NFTs) for valuable metals is a well-known example of assuring liquidity. NFTs that reflect ownership of a particular proportion of real-world assets, such as real estate, have the potential to demonstrate growth flexibility. Real estate agents might advertise properties as non-financial trusts (NFTs) with partial ownership of the assets.

As a consequence, numerous purchasers might potentially acquire a share in a single asset provided specific requirements are met. Finally, the promise of future royalty payments to creators via NFTs has significant ramifications for future growth, particularly crucial. While NFTs provide tremendous benefits to various players in the system, they also have the potential to give some broader benefits to all participants. For example, NFTs effectively generate inclusive growth, as shown by the many application cases of NFTs in various industries.

Unquestionably, the NFT blockchain technology offers a wide range of benefits that make it a very profitable investment. They provide incredible advantages not just to the inventors but also to the resellers who use them. There is significant potential for NFTs to become a vital component of the destiny of most sectors in the foreseeable future. In conclusion, non-fungible tokens (NFTs) are helpful to consumers in many ways. However, although NFT requires more exploration in terms of issues such as application, cyber security, and exploitation, it has already established itself to be a viable method that might be adopted by a variety of industries in the future.

CHAPTER NO. 5
HOW TO CREATE NFT?

NATHAN REAL

Chapter No. 5
How to Create NFT?

Despite the fact that NFTs are often sold and purchased using cryptocurrencies like Ethereum and Bitcoin, they are not themselves cryptocurrency. Cryptocurrencies are fungible in the same way that dollars and other commodities are. If you swap a single bitcoin for another bitcoin, the value of both bitcoins remains the same, and you'll still have one bitcoin in your possession. Due to the fact that NFTs are one-of-a-kind, they have no monetary worth other than what the customers are willing to pay for them.

5.1 Selecting an Item

Select an item from the list. Let us begin with the fundamentals. If you've not already done so, you'll have to figure out what kind of one-of-a-kind digital item you'd want to convert into an NFT. It may be anything from bespoke artwork to photographs, music, video game collectibles, memes, GIFs, or tweets. An NFT is a one-of-a-kind digital artifact with a single owner, and the item's rarity contributes to its NFT value. In order to convert an item into an NFT, you must first ensure that you control the intellectual property of the object. If you create an NFT for a virtual digital asset that you do not own, you may find yourself in legal danger. Picking the artwork is the first and most crucial step you must take. Non-fungible tokens may describe any digital file that is not fungible. Making an NFT of digital painting, a text, a piece of music, or a video may be done in many ways. Anything that may be duplicated as a media file is considered a multimedia file. After all, the goal of the NFT game is to transform digital artwork into "unique" items in an era when everything may be replicated indefinitely.

5.2 Selecting Blockchain

Select the blockchain that you want to use. Once you've chosen your one-of-a-kind digital asset, it's time to begin the procedure of minting it into a non-fungible token. The first step is identifying the blockchain technology you wish to utilize for your NFT. Ethereum is the most appreciated cryptocurrency among NFT artists and producers (CRYPTO: ETH). Cosmos, Tezos, Polkadot, and Binance Smart Chain are other prominent cryptocurrencies.

5.3 Supply of Ether

Have a supply of Ether on hand. Following the selection of your digital asset, the next step is to get some Ether. Assume for the sake of simplification that you're going to use Ethereum to create your NFTs, but there are a variety of blockchains you may choose from. That is the most widely used, and it is supported by the majority of the most notable NFT markets.

It may be necessary to spend money in order to mint an NFT. As a result, you will want an Ethereum wallet with some Ethers (the funds based on Ethereum). "MetaMask" is one of the simplest to utilize among the available options. Your Android smartphone or iPhone may be equipped with the app, which is entirely free. The price at which the NFT is asked to be created is quite changeable. Ensure that you have at least 100$ worth of Ether, but keep in mind that the minting procedure might cost you significantly more, depending on the daily operating price of the cryptocurrency.

If you want to mint the NFT on OpenSea, however, the procedure is entirely free of cost due to the sort of token the system will generate; nonetheless, you will still require to link your wallet to establish an account.

5.4 Account Creation

Create an account using your digital wallet. If you still do not have a digital payment wallet, you will need to establish one to finance the creation of your NFT since you will need bitcoin to fund your first investment. You will be able to access your digital assets via the use of the wallet. Metamask, Trust Wallet, AlphaWallet, Math wallet, and Coinbase Wallet are the best NFT wallets available. After you've created your digital wallet, you'll want to go out and purchase some bitcoin. The cryptocurrency Ether, which is used by the Ethereum blockchain platform, is accepted by the majority of NFT sites. If you already have cryptocurrency in another wallet, you'll want to link it to your digital wallet so that you may use it to make and trade NFTs. If you don't currently have cryptocurrency, you'll want to connect it as soon as possible.

5.5 Selecting NFT Market

Select your preferred NFT market. When you have a digital wallet and a small amount of bitcoin, it is time to begin generating (and, perhaps, selling) your own NFT token. An NFT marketplace will be required in order to complete your transaction in this manner. OpenSea, Axie Marketplace, Larva Labs/CryptoPunks, NBA Biggest Shot Marketplace, Rarible, Mintable, SuperRare, Foundation, Nifty Gateway, and Theta Drop are just a few of the top NFT marketplaces. You'll need to do thorough research into each NFT marketplace to choose a platform that is a suitable match for your business. Examples include Axie Marketplace, which serves as the online storefront for the popular NFT game Axie Infinity.

On the other hand, NBA Top Shot is a marketplace only focused on basketball. It's also crucial to know that specific markets have their own money that must be used on their platform. Rarible, for example, necessitates the use of Rarible (CRYPTO: RARI). OpenSea is an excellent location to start most of the time. It enables you to mint your own NFT, and it is the market leader in NFT distribution. In August 2021 alone, the NFT market sold NFTs valued at $3.4 billion. It will be necessary to link your NFT marketplace to your digital wallet when you have chosen one. This will let you pay the costs required to mint your NFT and keep any sales revenues in your possession.

Select a shopping center.

After completing your setup, you will need to choose a market where you will actually (virtually?) construct and then list your newfound wealth (NFT). The most popular of them are Mintable, Rarible, and OpenSea, to name a few. For the sake of this section, we'll use the last option since it's free to register, and there is no restriction on the material that may be listed. This implies that you do not need to be authorized as an artist to sell your work on the site. However, this also means that the marketplace is overflowing with digital trinkets that no one will ever use or purchase.

On OpenSea, choose "My Profile" from the drop-down menu under the user icon. On this screen, you may decide how you want to link your Ethereum wallet in order to continue. Connecting MetaMask to the platform is as simple as clicking on WalletConnect after choosing "Use a different wallet." If you're using another wallet, you can link it to the platform by selecting "Use a different Wallet" and then clicking on WalletConnect. In most cases, the method is uncomplicated. Proceed as the platform directs before confirming the Wallet Connect action via your MetaMask application.

5.6 Saving File

Save your file to your computer. You've finally arrived at the point where you can mint your NFT. A step-by-step tutorial for submitting your digital file to your selected NFT marketplace should be available on their website. Using this technique, you will be able to convert your digital file (an MP3, PNG, GIF, or another file type) into an NFT that is ready to be sold.

5.7 Including Description

Please include a description of your NFT to sell it. Adding a description and title to your listing is now available to you. Take some time to think about this to increase your NFT's likelihood of selling well. After that, you'll be asked to decide what proportion of royalties you'd want to receive from any future selling of your artwork. Increasing your proportion of sales will earn you more money in the long term, but doing so will discourage others from reselling your work in the first place since they will be less likely to earn a profit for themselves as a result of doing so. Finally, there is an optional box where you may enter the characteristics of your file. You'll be virtually finished after you've completed this task.

5.8 Profit

So, you've produced an NFT and successfully posted it on the OpenSea marketplace. What's the next step? What should I do now? Waiting for someone to notice your valuable token won't get you very far in this game. Unless you already have a group of individuals who might be enthusiastic about your work, you'll have to sell the thing yourself. That is the most challenging aspect of the process, and it has nothing to do with the creative endeavor itself. Yes, it is every bit as brutal and picky as the actual art world in which it exists. It's not a good idea unless you're the protagonist of a meme or other online phenomena. If that's the case, congratulations: you've most likely discovered a method to monetize that awful photo that others have always used to make a mockery of you.

5.9 Sales Procedure

Establish the sales procedure. To complete the NFT minting process, you must determine how to commercialize your non-fungible tokens (NFT). Depending on the system, you may do the following:

- Sell it at a predetermined price: By establishing a fixed price for your NFT, you will let the first individual interested in meeting that price purchase it.

- A timed auction will provide individuals interested in your NFT with a certain amount of time in which to place their final offer for the item at hand.

- Start an auction with an infinite number of bidders: A public auction is one in which there is no time restriction. Instead, you have the authority to call a halt to the auction at any time.

You'll need to decide on a starting price (if you're holding an auction), the number of royalties you'll get if your NFT is resold on the secondary marketplace, and how long you'll conduct the auction for (if timed). It's important to keep fees in mind while determining the minimum price since if you set the price too low, you might lose money on your NFT sale.

Unfortunately, the expenses associated with minting and selling an NFT may be prohibitively expensive and complicated. You may have to pay a listing charge, an NFT minting cost, a premium on the sale, and a transaction fee in order to move money from the buyer's wallet to yours, depending on the platform and price. Fees might also change due to the volatility in the value of cryptocurrencies. As a result, it's critical to carefully consider the expenses associated with minting and selling your NFT to ensure that they're helpful in the long run before proceeding.

Making NFTs may be a financially rewarding endeavor.

As NFTs become more popular, the prices at which they are sold increase. As a result, those developing NFTs stand to gain a great deal of money. In reality, given the high costs of minting and marketing NFTs, hardly all of them will ever sell, much alone generate revenue for their creators. Because of the expenditures, you must plan for the chance of incurring a financial loss due to your NFT production. Ensure that you sell an NFT that others would find helpful and that you establish a minimum value that will more than cover any related costs if you want to avoid a loss.

Follow the instructions provided by the NFT platform.

In order to generate a non-fungible token on an NFT marketplace, authors must follow particular procedures that are exclusive to that marketplace.

First and foremost, the marketplace often requires users to submit a file they want to be converted into an NFT, along with a title and a brief description. In terms of attracting collectors and optimizing their opportunity to sell their inventions, users of the NFT platform should spend some time filling out the specifics of their non-fungible tokens and refining them before launching their campaigns. Following the upload of the digital object, users will be required to pick whether to mint a token or a group of tickets from it.

Second, when selling NFTs, two alternatives are available: a predetermined price or an auction. A fixed-price sale is when customers select a price at which they wish to trade the NFT in question, and it is pretty straightforward and unambiguous. Using auctions to sell NFT inventions is another fascinating method of doing so. On most NFT markets, there are two kinds of auctions offered to participants. The first auction is an English auction, a bidding process where the highest bidder wins after the auction. The term "timed auction" refers to an English auction in which each lot may be bid on over a predetermined period. After that, the collector with the top bid wins and purchases a non-financial transaction (NFT). The second sort of auction is a Dutch auction, also referred to as a reducing auction, in which the cost of an NFT declines until someone buys it from the auctioneer.

Increasing the number of NFTs

Users may decide whether or not to advertise their newly minted NFT invention aggressively. The development of an NFT will depend on the user's NFT characteristics. The following are some fundamentals to which artists should pay attention: knowing their audience, developing a practical marketing approach, etc.

When it comes to marketing your NFT collection, one of the most effective approaches is brand awareness, which refers to building a good reputation in the market by disseminating positive news about you and your NFT collection.

Additionally, it might be marketed via internet advertising, such as publishing in specialist publications and appearances on cryptocurrency podcasts and social media marketing.

Since members can access the connections to their digital resources and the NFT marketplace's social media, it would make sense for creators to appeal to the biggest crowd possible if they are looking for the most avid collectors. Using social media to reach a large audience could be highly beneficial for creators. Users may create personal profiles on social media platforms like Twitter, Telegram, and Discord to advertise their NFTs, build a reputation, and raise public awareness. Twitter, Telegram, and Discord have already developed communication channels for the crypto community. As a result, they may meet some influential people and artists with whom they might cooperate and journalists from prominent publications interested in writing about them and their NFT collection.

Growing a dedicated community of NFT creators may be essential for marketing their products since these individuals will consistently support them, pass the message about them, invest in them, and readily purchase their NFT creations.

CHAPTER NO. 6

HOW TO MONETIZE YOUR NFT?

NATHAN REAL

Chapter No. 6
How to Monetize Your NFT?

People are becoming wealthy as a result of the NFT market. From Beeple's $69 million sales of his works of art, Everdays, to merely flipping collectibles, monetizing non-financial assets is all about placing your investment opportunities to work and allowing technology to help you grow your financial wealth. Moreover, with the NFT industry growing faster at 18,000 percent in just 12 months, the possibilities for monetization are becoming increasingly numerous. Because of NFTs, you can turn your art, music, photography, and even your duration into money by implementing the appropriate strategy. Some of the tools and best practices of NFT revenues for NFT creators will be discussed below, as will a little more unconventional methods that should not be ruled out.

6.1 Digital Paintings and Collectibles Creation

Create beautiful works of digital painting and collectibles that people want to own. One of the most apparent but time-tested methods of earning revenue from non-profit organizations is to start creating artwork that people are interested in purchasing with platforms such as OpenSea generating and over two million sales per month, finding a viewer for your photographs, painting, animations, digital sketch or video is now easier than it has ever b Companies are knocking on the door of artists like Fewocious' to collaborate with them. They have gone from drawing in class and on their iPad to becoming multi-millionaires. Non-financial monetization here simply entails the creation of art that others are self-assured in investing in. Early adopters of Fewocious' artwork recognized the potential in his work, and they now realize the rewards of their investment. Similarly, NFT investors are interested in collaborating with other artists. However, while the attraction of art and collectibles is highly subjective, there are some characteristics that all influential NFT creators have in common.

6.2 Preserve the Presence of Scarcity

For starters, they don't overindulge in creative endeavors. By exclusively minting genuinely exceptional NFT art, you can guarantee that your following connects you with high-quality NFT artwork. This shortage should translate into restricted production runs, limiting the amount of product available. To feel as though they have discovered the next great thing, investors must believe they have. If your restricted supply totals thousands of units, they'll be less inclined to buy from you. Instead, keep your NFT runs limited, with just a little quantity of money being minted. Additionally, you may generate fake rarity by pricing distinct varieties of an NFT in different ways. Investors will better understand their investment if the levels are described in terms of rarity, ranging from ordinary to exceptional to ultra-rare.

6.3 Be Easily Identifiable

Maintaining a focus on one or two channels is also essential. Subscribers are interested in knowing where they may locate your work. For example, by exclusively minting and displaying artwork on a platform like OpenSea, you'll not only boost your likelihood with the platform's algorithm – which will put your work in front of as many people – but you'll also see more traffic sent your way from other websites and social media.

6.4 Visibility of Work

Make Your Work More Visible. It's pointless to work on the next NFT masterwork and keep it a secret from the rest of the world. Use your social media networks to direct consumers to your preferred platforms and begin transactions. It is critical to ensure that your postings have the appropriate tags. Investment professionals routinely utilize hashtags such as #nftcollectors and just #nfts to find new and emerging art and collectibles.

Additionally, you may utilize a site like Lazy.com to exhibit your work, which will let you quickly and efficiently connect to a portfolio of your NFTs. The addresses of these cards may be correlated to wallet addresses in order to make transactions.

6.5 Collect NFT Royalty Payments

Traditional works of art are created to understand that after the item has been ordered and the transaction has been completed, the artist effectively relinquishes all ownership rights in the work. All of this is different with NFTs. Artists may sell a piece of work and continue to get royalties from subsequent sales in perpetuity. This implies that even if the NFT has changed ownership numerous times over the course of five or ten years, the original artist will still be able to benefit from their work of art. Even though ownership has been abandoned, NFTs nonetheless enable artists to profit from a rise in the value of their work.

In order to maintain a persistent and immutable track of all finances and ownership, blockchain technology must be used. The royalties are something that the artist may benefit from throughout the NFT. Still, they are also automated, so there is no risk of them being misallocated, as the music business is in the film industry. With platforms like OpenSea and Rarible, a royalty plan is generally an opt-in option, allowing for a customizable percentage of kickback, up to 10%, to be received. Royalties are then given to the original author by the platforms once a month, and they may be retrieved at that time.

Consider the following scenario: an NFT developer mints a set of ten collectibles with a 10 percent royalty that quickly gains appeal within the investment community. Each NFT has initially been sold for 0.5 ETH in the first auction. The value of the NFTs increases with time, and one of the collectibles is now selling for 3 ETH. This equates to 0.3 ETH being returned to the originator. The identical item sells for 5 ETH on the same website six months later. The investor earns a 10 percent royalty for 0.5 ETH, which is the second time the creator has received a royalty.

Without royalty, the artists would have earned a single payment of 0.5 ETH, which would have been insufficient to cover expenses. Because of the implementation of the royalty structure, NFT monetization can generate continuous and sustained revenue from previous works.

6.6 Flip Collectibles

Flipping your assets is also an excellent technique to monetize NFTs if you have more money than you can use to develop. If you keep an eye out for the following extensive collection, you may make ten-fold earnings in a short period of time. Specimen collections like Pudgy Penguins, which include 8,888 different penguin character tokens, have witnessed significant increases in value in only a few short months. Several tokens initially worth 0.1 Eth are now worth ten times that amount, with more gains predicted in the future.

Identifying popular in the NFT market is more art than a science, taking practice. The process includes a certain amount of speculation, some leap of faith, and a grasp of what distinguishes NFTs from other types of financial instruments. Specifically, scarcity and anything that has the potential to become fashionable.

The key is to be engaged in the NFT group, continue reading, talking, and surf the markets. CryptoPunks were first given out freely to the first 10,000 persons who signed up. Some of those jerks are now worth more than $11 million, making individuals who took advantage of the situation enormously wealthy.

An established technique is to purchase NFTs in volume from online markets and then advertise them separately on the platform. However, even though it is more time-consuming, doing this process on a regular basis might result in significant gains. Decentraland's LAND parcels, for example, are often sold as a group on online auction websites. Reclassifying these plots and selling them separately will usually result in a profitable transaction.

6.7 Non-Linear Fractional Function

Construct a Non-Linear Fractional Function (NFT). The use of platforms such as Fractional. Art to fractionalize a valuable NFT and allow its popularity and interest to enhance its value is a modern method of monetizing a valued NFT. When you fractionalize NFTs, you effectively divide them into parts that may be utilized for various DeFi applications in the form of ERC-20 tokens. As a consequence of this split ownership, it is feasible for numerous parties to possess a single NFT, resulting in increased liquidity in the marketplace. This is a very profitable option for creating or owning a non-profit organization. The most well-known example of NFT fractionalization is presently the original Doge meme, which was auctioned as an NFT for $4 million in June 2021, making it the most valuable NFT ever sold. The NFT's owner, PleasrDAO, decided to divide the NFT into millions of tokens, letting everyone become a part-owner of the cryptocurrency. The price of the NFT skyrocketed to $45 million at the inaugural auction, and the total project is currently worth more than $302 million. Ownership of the lion's share of the ERC-20 tokens and witnessing their value develop has proven to be very advantageous for PleasrDAO.

6.8 Non-Fielding Tools

Make Use of Your Non-Fielding Tools (NFTs). An example of one of the most inventive methods of monetizing NFT is via the game Axie Infinity. The game generated $364 million in sales in August 2021 alone, an increase of 85 percent over the previous month, exhibiting remarkable growth. Obtaining Axie NFTs and then lending money to individuals who will pay the owner back in tokens known as Smooth Love Potions is one method of generating income from Axie NFTs (SLP). Axies, like Pokemon, differ in terms of their power and traits. To get started, you'll need a group of three people, and some participants won't be able to put in the necessary funds.

Consequently, both the athlete and the owner of Axie NFTs stand to gain by participating in the Axie scholarship program. Essentially, an Axie "scholar" is a player leased to a club by a scholarship manager in exchange for earning SLP on their behalf. The earnings are settled upon in advance, for example, a 50/50 split, a 60/40 split, and so on.

The SLP tokens may then be traded on exchanges and marketplaces for fiat cash, or they can be retained in a digital wallet and sold when the value of the tokens rises.

Not only does the scenario benefit the player and the owner, but it also helps the whole community. As a consequence of the scholarship program, the game's popularity continues to rise, resulting in an increase in SLP price.

CHAPTER NO. 7
NFT MARKETPLACES

NATHAN REAL

Chapter No. 7
NFT Marketplaces

You will see that NFT markets are a vital element of the fascinating new trend of NFTs, which you can read more about here. NFT markets have made it simpler and more flexible for people to access NFTs while also addressing long-standing difficulties with income streams for authors. However, the debate on non-financial-transaction markets eventually boils down to one topic. NFT artists and purchasers would undoubtedly seek solutions to the question "what is the greatest NFT marketplace?" to maximize their creations' value. Although these sites and others are home to hundreds of NFT makers and collectors, ensure that the place is correct before purchasing. Some artists have fallen prey to cosplayers who have advertised and marketed their work without their consent. Most importantly, the rapid expansion of various non-financial-transaction (NFT) markets is a significant source of worry. In this situation, a clear sketch of some of the most well-known NFT markets, together with a detailed explanation, may be beneficial.

Here is a list of some of the most well-known NFT markets that may be of use to you as you explore new territory in the NFT world.

7.1 OpenSea

According to current industry standards, OpenSea is not only the most significant NFT marketplace, but it is also the biggest of the NFT markets in the world. It offers a wide range of non-fungible token kinds, including art, virtual worlds, censorship-resistant domain names, souvenirs, sports, and trading cards, among other things. This peer-to-peer marketplace brands itself a provider of "rare digital objects and collectibles." All you have to do is set up an account to explore NFT collections to get started. You may also arrange works by sales volume to find new artists. OpenSea integrates assets with the ERC1155 and ERC721 cryptographic standards are noteworthy. Purchase, sell and discover unique digital assets such as Axies, Decentraland, CryptoKitties (as well as ENS names), and other digital assets using this platform. Over 700 projects of all types, including trading card games, digital art projects, name systems like the Ethereum Name Service (ENS), and collectible games, are shown on OpenSea. The item mining function on OpenSea is also one of the marketplace's most notable features as a non-traditional trading platform. Designers can build their things and establish their NFT collection using the minting tool. Those designing their intelligent contracts for digital collectibles or games will find OpenSea the ideal marketplace for them.

7.2 The Nifty Gateway

Nifty Gateway is the most likely candidate to answer the question, "What is the greatest NFT marketplace? "It is without a doubt one of the most reputable high-end NFT markets for dealing in crypto-art works. The collaboration of Nifty Gateway with leading producers, companies, athletes, and artists is beneficial to the company. To be more specific, the cooperation offers crypto art collectors the opportunity to acquire just one-of-a-kind pieces of artwork. On the other hand, it is pretty tough to get approved on the Nifty Gateway when it comes to crypto art markets. As a result, prominent artists, corporations, and celebrity makers are able to get access to this online platform. Three main auction methods are

Nifty Gateway also provides royalties since artists may choose the proportion of secondary sales. As a leading non-financial transaction platform, it accepts debit cards, credit cards, and ether (ETH) payments.

7.3 SuperRare

The NFT marketplace SuperRare is yet another intriguing NFT marketplace that comes to mind while thinking about the most acceptable alternatives. The website is primarily focused on functioning as a marketplace where users may trade in one-of-a-kind pieces of digital art that have been produced in limited quantities. An artist that is a member of the SuperRare network creates original artwork. The platform tokenizes the painting and makes it available as a crypto asset or collectible, owned and traded like any other asset. Many industry professionals commend SuperRare for introducing a fresh approach to online connection with culture, art, and collecting unlike anything else available. The emergence of a social network during the SuperRare marketplace is the game's most notable aspect. Because digital collectibles are coupled with visible ownership documentation, they may be appropriate for use in a social setting.

SuperRare is appropriate for beginning artists with a natural aptitude for invention and inventiveness. It is compatible with Ether, which is the native coin of the Ethereum blockchain.

7.4 Rarible

It would be impossible to have a debate about the leading NFT marketplace without mentioning the word Rarible. It is a fundamental and easy-to-use NFT platform with few barriers to entry for artists looking to establish themselves. As a result, folks who are just getting their feet wet in the world of NFT may find Rarible to be quite beneficial. Like OpenSea, Rarible is a democratic, open marketplace that enables artists and producers to issue and sell NFTs. RARI tokens created on the platform let holders vote on features like charges and community rules. Despite this, the user experience is somewhat hampered by a jumbled layout, contributing to the overall negative impression. The most intriguing aspect of Rarible is that it has its cryptocurrency, RARI. RARI is a valuable tool for rewarding platform users engaged on the platform. The Ethereum blockchain charges 2.5 percent in transaction fees on every sale. It accepts a variety of cryptocurrencies, including WITH, ATRI, and DAI, in addition to RARI and ETH. Furthermore, Rarible is a dependable non-financial-transaction (NFT) marketplace for royalties since artists may choose the percentage of earnings they wish to receive from secondary sales.

7.5 Foundation

Foundation is one of the most significant newcomers to the NFT markets that has garnered headlines in recent weeks and months. It has emerged as the most reliable non-financial transaction platform for many crypto art makers. The ability to create collections curated by community members is a distinguishing feature of the Foundation. Creators and collectors alike may encourage young artists to join the Foundation via a collaborative approach. Here, creators must earn "upvotes" or invite other creators to share their paintings. The community's exclusivity and expense of entry—artists must also acquire "gas" to mint NFTs—means it may feature higher-caliber artwork. For instance, Nyan Cat inventor Chris Torres sold the NFT on the Foundation platform. It may also imply higher pricing – not entirely a bad thing for collectors and artists trying to profit if the market for NFTs continues at present levels or even grows over time. As a result, creators will have easy access to the "Creator Invites" function after they have sold their first NFT. Foundation is a good option for any artist who can create a mark and distinguish themselves as a unique creation. It accepts payments in Ether and promises to provide new functionality that will ensure a 10 percent royalty on all secondary sales in the near future.

7.6 Cargo

Many excellent competitors go undiscovered among the strong players who may be found as the most acceptable option for an NFT marketplace and are so overlooked. Cargo is an example of inclusion on this list that would be an excellent pick for any newcomer to the NFT area. It accepts payments in the cryptocurrency Ether and enables anybody to submit an application. The most noticeable aspect of Cargo is that it does not include any auctions for non-ferrous metals. Pricing selections are entirely up to the discretion of the artists. It also makes it possible to use the 'Split Royalties' function, which adds up to 15 different Ethereum wallet addresses. The answer to the question, "What is the greatest NFT marketplace?" might also lead you to Cargo, which is a marketplace that is simple to use. Creators of NFTs may benefit from trustworthy and cost-effective techniques to get started with NFT trading and mining. Cargo's 'Magic Minting' function also assists in avoiding petrol surcharges, demonstrating the utility of this feature in terms of cost-effectiveness.

7.7 Myth Market

Despite the fact that there isn't much to say about Myth Market, it is essential to note that it is not a single NFT marketplace. Myth Market is a collection of online markets that are both versa and simple to use and handle. The Myth Market now has numerous significant highlights, like GPK Market, Heroes Market, Shatner Market, Pepe Market, and KOGS Market, to name just a few. Each of the listed marketplaces is distinct in the collectible brands re-presented—for instance, the GPK. The market enables you to tra-de Garbage Pail Kids trading cards with other people. As a result, it is easy to see that Myth Market provides a realistic picture of the potential of non-traditional markets in the future.

7.8 Mintable

Mintable would have been a necessary addition to the NFT mar-kets list for 2021. It performs the function of a complete NFT marketplace, allowing users to trade nearly everything from art to music to video game stuff to rare treasures. One of the most pro-mising aspects of Mintable is the gasless minting option, which is also available. Based on the Ethereum blockchain, this auction platform accepts only Ethereum payments and offers three di-fferent auctions. A timed auction, a Buy It Now auction, and a traditional auction are among the available types. The option of royalties allows creators to receive a percentage of 5 percent of all secondary sales if they choose to do so through this method.

Mintable is undoubtedly the most recommended platform for an-yone interested in NFTs, particularly beginners.

7.9 Enjin

The term "Enjin Marketplace" is often used to refer to the finest NFT marketplace, and it is well-known in many circles. It has the potential to facilitate the exploration and exchange of blockchain assets. Enjin Marketplace, in particular, is the best option for En-jin-based non-financial transactions. As of now, it has recorded Enjin coin spending on digital purchases totaling over $43.8 mi-llion in Enjin coin value. According to some estimates, there are around 2.1 billion NFTs globally. The Enjin Wallet makes it sim-ple to list and purchase gaming collectibles and commodities and make payments. Enjin-based blockchain projects may be found on the 'Projects' tab, accessible to creators. Projects might include community-backed collectibles, game item collection, and gamified incentive schemes, among other things. Consequently, if you choose Enjin Marketplace as your favorite NFT marketplace, you will have an easier time finding perfect prospects.

7.10 Known Origin

The last addition on this list of NFT markets, KnownOrigin, is a specialist crypto art platform not included in the previous list. It presents creators with medium to high levels of difficulty in getting their work approved into the site. On the contrary, acceptance into KnownOrigin does not need authors to have a significant audience or to be recognized as established artists. When it comes to promoting artists, the KnownOrigin's 'Trending' feature is a promising method that may be used. A benefit of this feature is that it assists in displaying the identity and effort of creators in the KnownOrigin environment. However, artists with a distinct and genuine work portfolio are given favor on KnownOrigin, unquestionably a top NFT platform for newcomers. The Royalties for creators in the sum of 12.5 percent of secondary sales are paid out to them.

Finally, choosing the most significant NFT marketplace from among the several possibilities listed here in this section is tough. Every single inclusion on the list can meet the needs of a variety of distinct target groups. When it comes to translating their work into NFTs, new artists and well-accepted artists have very different tastes in terms of the format. In addition, there are differences in the concerns about royalties and expenses connected with non-financial transactions (NFT) on the markets.

You might choose the best marketplace if you have a clear understanding of the concept of NFT markets and instructions on how they operate. Identify your top options from among the most fabulous NFT markets and find out what you should do right now!

CHAPTER NO. 8
REAL STATES

NATHAN REAL

Chapter No. 8
Real Estates

We understand what you're thinking, and we agree. Who in their right state of mind would want to invest in virtual real estate, anyway? To be very honest, a large number of individuals are excited to acquire their piece of NFT real estate. According to the company, those interested in NFT real estate include collectors, gamers, investors, and even giant corporations. The potential that virtual land has is enormous! In order to sell pizza from their website, Dominos established a physical location and began accepting orders, and Nike is not far off.

8.1 What Is NFT Real Estate?

The growth of virtual real estate is being powered by an expansion of its scope, which is being generated by intriguing surroundings where people can speak with one another, shop, make money, and socialize just as they would in the real world, according to the trend. Untold individuals are becoming conscious of the enormous potential for company growth in the virtual world. According to the Associated Press, this is an area where many people are looking for investment and money-making possibilities. This is an excellent alternative to the actual world. Consumers were already purchasing virtual items to enhance their gaming experience in video games. Virtual reality allows you to engage with people, buy things, participate in activities, make money, and find companionship. Isn't it what we all desire from the world we live in? To add to that, the virtual world, which is a product of the imaginations of game designers and artists, is a fascinating creation. Everything is enjoyable, engaging, and entertaining. And now you've been given a chance to own a portion of this incredible universe. This seems to be a fantastic chance for many people. It's no surprise that a growing number of investors are opting to invest their wealth in our country. Businesses are shutting their doors in the actual world, and hotels are mostly vacant. People spend an increasing amount of time on the internet, and transactions are increasingly conducted online. So why not make an online investment?

In the NFT real estate market, there are several opportunities. According to a recent report, the land is built and sold in video games and virtual worlds. Virtual real estate seems to provide an almost limitless number of options. Cryptocurrency blockchain technology underpins digital transactions, ensuring that the virtual land is accurate and belongs to the rightful owner. The land piece that one owns is one-of-a-kind and cannot be duplicated. Once you have purchased a plot of land in the digital world, you are free to construct anything you wish on it. You can build a shop, a house, a company, and a community.

Because more and more individuals visit these other realms, you will commercialize it. When the virtual world grows more populous, landowners will be able to rent out their property, sell it, and swap it for other non-fungible tokens (NFTs). NFT Real Estate exists in the virtual world of the metaverse. Experts have examined the Metaverse to see if it has the potential to influence individuals, education, and research. The gaming industry has contributed to purchasing digitalized real estate and products. While participating in virtual reality video games, gamers may purchase objects to improve their in-game experience, such as virtual land, by using real money. It has become a valuable tool for doing commerce online because of the value of NFTs in assessing authenticity and ownership, which is based on blockchain technology. Because of the blockchain's ability to allow safe transactions, it seems that there is nothing that can prevent the gaming industry from putting virtual products and virtual real estate for sale shortly. At the moment, the Metaverse is a virtual shared area where individuals, symbolized by digital avatars, come together to establish communities, which grow and eventually build civilizations. Connecting virtual reality and augmented reality technologies with the virtual world transition seems to be a logical next step in developing these tools. Many people are becoming aware of this and are preparing to shift into the metaverse. Virtual worlds such as Decentraland and Cryptovoxels are now the most popular. Both worlds allow for the purchase of land parcels, which anyone may acquire for their future usage. Investors increasingly see virtual reality ventures as lucrative investments. Even state fund, established by Republic Real Estate Inc., is dedicated. In reality, as we make the digital revolution into the future, most people find much in the virtual world. There seems to be a significant potential emerging in these virtual environments. Many people believe that purchasing a plot of land and creating digital property is wise. According to the company, land prices in the virtual world Cryptovoxels surged from $800 to $3900 in the first 2-3 months of 2021. This is a tremendous boom, and there are several chances for individuals to profit handsomely from this development. The biggest concern is that one will lose out on this phenomenon. Buyers are snatching up the few spots, and the secondary marketplace is experiencing a rise in demand. Many people are gaining money by selling their properties at a higher price than they paid for them originally.

8.2 How to Purchase?

A fundamental way of buying NFT real estate consists of setting up a crypto-wallet and depositing the necessary cash, then accessing a marketplace that provides NFT properties for sale. The Decentraland Cryptovoxels Project is now open for business. In possible to purchase virtual land, and in virtual worlds, Decentraland and Cryptovoxels are two of the most famous virtual land alternatives available. Let's take a closer look at each of them individually.

Decentraland

Decentraland is a virtual environment based on the Ethereum blockchain and is currently under development. It might very quickly be referred regarded as a Cyber Utopia. People come to

Decentraland to buy, socialize, sell, and provide services to the community. MANA is the money used in Decentraland, and it can be exchanged for real-world cash in the same way that bitcoin can be exchanged for real-world currency. While it is not required to own property in Decentraland to visit, now is a perfect moment to possibly chase a plot of land to benefit in the nearby. Their NFT property has been subdivided is now available for purchase in pieces. Each land parcel represents a non-fungible token (NFT) on the blockchain. This signifies that it is one-of-a-kind, unchangeable, and irreplaceable. This is analogous to real estate in the actual world, except it is much simpler to get owing to NFTs and blockchain technology. Land may be purchased, sold, or rented by anybody in this area. To buy land on Decentraland, you may do so using an Ethereum marketplace like OpenSea. You will get a land token with specific coordinates to a particular site on the platform. In addition, Metamask will be required to purchase and sell land in Decentraland. After you have purchased the property, you can either rent it out or sell it at an auction to the winning bidder for a profit. You may also use your land by establishing a business or constructing a residence. The amount of land accessible here is restricted, just like in real life. The overall land area consists of 43689 private property parcels, 33886 district parcels, 9438 highways, and 3588 plazas. It is a square plot of land measuring 16m by 16m in size. You may check out the current real estate rates on the official OpenSea or the Decentraland Marketplace, and both are hosted on Decentraland. The official Decentraland market accepts MANA as a form of payment. However, you may also use Ethereum if you like. OpenSea provides the possibility to purchase virtual land all using ETH and MANA cryptocurrency.

Cryptovoxels

People feel that Cryptovoxels is a combination of Facebook and Minecraft and prefer it to Decentraland. Cryptovoxel packages are also available for purchase on OpenSea. The Cryptovoxel packages have six different dimensions, and these measurements describe the precise location of the piece of land inside the Cryptovoxel universe. Cryptovoxel is a term that is slowly rising in use.

Approximately 80 percent of the land that has been sold has been created. The geographic center of this universe – a metropolis known as Origin city — is a typical city, complete with streets, businesses, and residences. To pay a visit, browse the Cryptovoxel website and then choose particular geographical locations from the drop-down box on the left. If you find a piece of land you like, you may select it and buy it using your Metamask digital wallet. Cryptovoxels is a highly user-friendly platform to create things. Once you have been granted permission, you will be able to access a builder panel, where you will discover a variety of settings to aid you with the construction. You may begin constructing right in your browser, and you can add color, photos, and even audio files as you go.

You are no longer need to own anything at all to attend and observe. Cryptovoxels gives non-transferable tokens (NFT) packages to ensure that nothing can be falsified or stolen. Transactions are in NFTs, which are then kept on the Ethereum blockchain. Cryptovoxels are plots of land that have been assigned unique coordinates for particular places.

In contrast to Decentraland, there are no set sizes to which you are restricted. The majority of folks either acquire their land or purchase newly constructed homes. Cryptovoxels platforms are suitable with virtual reality devices such as the Oculus Quest, the Oculus Rift, and others. These devices will aid in connecting the physical world with the digital world, and a great deal of work has been done in this area.

Because everything is done in the browser, you don't need any coding knowledge to complete the project. It functions on a block-based system for everything. All you have to do is drag and drop the bricks to assemble your package. The proceeds from the sale of the plots will go toward supporting the Cryptovoxel development.

Others

Some other crypto-based worlds, such as Axe infinity, Somnium Space, and The Sandbox, are also witnessing a growth in the number of members and visitors to their respective communities.

8.3 Investing in NFT Real Estate

Owning NFT real estate may appear to be an impossible dream, but is it? For example, a large number of individuals have already purchased virtual land. Certain assets, maps, and one-of-a-kind objects are available for purchase in popular online games, but they have a cost. So, should you invest in NFT real estate by purchasing your piece?

Suppose you're an investor, collector, or player who wants access to a range of various land alternatives as well as the possibility of earning a return on your investment. In that case, you should consider owning NFT real estate (virtual land). Buying NFT real estate, particularly in the initial stage, is likely a wise decision, as the property's value and demand for these virtual parcels continue to climb as the development progresses. Although the most virtual property is priced at a premium, this does not rule out the possibility of purchasing your portion of NFT real estate. Given that virtual real estate is just starting to gain popularity, investing in the sector now might result in significant rewards in the future. This scenario, which incorporates virtual reality, bitcoin, and blockchain technology, provides a hopeful new outlook of virtual land and assets in general. On the other hand, owing to the unknowable certainty that the future contains, predicting whether acquiring a virtual parcel will pay off in the future. So, remember to weigh the advantages and disadvantages of having your virtual real estate property before deciding.

There are several advantages to owning virtual real estate:

- Investing in virtual real estate may be a wise decision.

- Virtual real estate provides opportunities to establish enterprises, communities, and social relationships with other people.

- NFT real estate may be purchased in a secure and hassle-free manner with no risk of fraud.

The disadvantages of possessing virtual real estate:

- Virtual real estate is not a cost-effective alternative to traditional real estate for some individuals.

- Uncertainty surrounds the future of the virtual real estate.

- There is no assurance that the blockchain you acquire your property will continue to be supported shortly.

After weighing the advantages and disadvantages, you'll have to determine if purchasing your own NFT real estate is a worthwhile investment. If you are someone who expects to profit simply from the ownership of virtual property, you may be frustrated in the future, as many others are. That is why it is critical to investigate any virtual property before purchasing it. On the other hand, purchasing any virtual property that appeals to you is a sensible option if you are a collector or an enthusiast. Financial incentives do not just drive the desire for NFT real estate. People who engage in virtual worlds or video games find that virtual worlds may help them meet their social requirements. This is one of the reasons why an increasing number of individuals are signing up for these sites. With NFT real estate, we see an unprecedented window of opportunity. Are you ready to take on the world?

8.4 Why Will NFT Real Estate Worth Increase?

NFTs are doing incredibly well, as seen by the news of the multiple high-priced transactions that have been reported. As interest in NFTs grows, the demand for NFT-related real estate will soar. Because virtual land is administered on the blockchain, the level of security is excellent, and many consider it to be a relatively risk-free investment opportunity. Even mortgages on NFT real estate are permissible under certain circumstances. Furthermore, digital worlds are not a new idea; they have been there for a long time and were made famous by websites such as Eve Online and second life, to name a few examples. Players had created sophisticated economies in these digital environments, rising in popularity as time went on.

Even though individuals did go to these realms, most of their actions and experiences were in the actual world. The lockdown and epidemic of 2020 were a watershed moment in human history, prompting individuals to interact more online than in person. In turn, this has resulted in a massive worldwide shift to virtual worlds, which has significantly raised the price of NFT real estate in general. Because of the increase in visitors to these gaming and virtual sites, investors and collectors alike have become more aware of the possibilities and potential implicit in the NFT real estate boom. Some individuals are willing to spend large sums of bitcoin to purchase parcels strategically. This is the future, and they are determined to be a part of it as soon as they are allowed to participate. Once they have gained access to these platforms, they are anxious to begin building, renting, or flipping properties for a profit.

CHAPTER NO. 9

BECOMING A CRYPTOARTIST

NATHAN REAL

Chapter No. 9
Becoming a CryptoArtist

For newcomers, learning what an NFT is furthermore, digital relatively straightforward, but one of the most frequently asked questions, with ambiguous answers, is: "How do I become a CryptoArtist?" Throughout this, you'll go over the fundamentals of being a CryptoArtist.

9.1 The Technical Part

The first step is, of course, to open a cryptocurrency wallet and convert fiat currencies (such as US dollars or British pounds sterling) into the cryptocurrency Ethereum. To tokenize your works of art on NFT stores, you'll need to have ETH on hand.

9.2 Familiarity with NFT Stores

Be familiar with the various NFT stores. One type of NFT store is a general NFT store, where everyone can sell their work of art, and the other is a curated store, where artists must first be accepted before they can sell their work. OpenSea and Rarible are the two popular NFT stores, but others, such as Cargo and Mintable, are also popular. Platforms such as Marketplace, KnownOrigin, SuperRare, Nifty Gateway, and Blockparty vet the artists before allowing them to sell their work and require an application. Getting accepted into these groups can be challenging if you're a newcomer with little or no social media presence.

9.3 Connection with Others

Make contact with other members of your tribe through the CryptoTwitter community. This is the most effective method of getting began as a CryptoArtist. Connecting with other creators and collectors in the New Frontiers of Technology (NFT) arena is an essential component of marketing and selling your work. In addition to Twitter, there are many Discord groups and a few tiny Facebook communities where most of the activity occurs. Twitter is a more convenient way to get started and interact with people, and you can learn about Discord groups by following them on Twitter. The clubhouse has also lately gained popularity as a gathering place for members of the NFT community.

Explore artists on marketplaces such as marketplace, KnownOrigin, and follow those who strike a chord with you on Twitter. From there, you can easily fall down the rabbit hole of other people's retweets and tags, which will lead you to more artists. And don't forget to interact with the general public! Collaborate with the artists, fans, and collectors in order to develop long-lasting connections with them. Comment on the pieces of art you appreciate, express your thoughts and solicit comments from the creators.

9.4 Know Yourself

Be Aware of Your Personality. It should go without stating, but it is critical to be aware of your particular style and distinguish yourself from the crowd as an artist. Just a handful of artists can readily be differentiated from the others based on a single glance at their works of art. Understand your company's brand style and message.

9.5 Increasing Value of Collection

Increase the value of the collection for the collectors. A deluge of short-term, quick-flip initiatives is now inundating the CryptoArt field, with little prospect of retaining their worth in the long run. Even while there is no simple answer to what owners and investors desire, it is reasonable to say that they like to purchase works from artists who can promote themselves and expand in the area, as well as those who are likely to be there for the long haul. It's usually a good idea to add value and intrigue to a portfolio by offering something unique to long-term investors, such as limited-time reductions. Collectors also like scarcity and exclusivity, such as the knowledge that they possess a one-of-a-kind edition or a special artwork with only ten copies in total.

9.6 Advertise Your Art

Bring Your Art to the Attention of the World. Never be afraid to shill (which is slang for "show off/promote") your artwork! Like physical art, marketing is a critical component of selling your digital art. Additionally, with the increasing number of artists entering the space, it is becoming increasingly crucial. Suppose you're selling via OpenSea or Rarible. In that case, you'll have to rely totally on your marketing skills since those are generic markets for everyone and everyone. You'll have to work hard to ensure that as many people see your artworks, make a list of the social media outlets that are most relevant for your profession, and don't be afraid to join organizations or advertise yourself on Twitter, but don't go overboard with it. You will bring more attention to your CryptoArt profile through your social media activity. If you want to establish credibility and a "brand image" for your work, a portfolio and website are also essential tools to have. Most CryptoArt platforms will request that you submit a portfolio, so it's always a good idea to have one available.

Additionally, having a website will help prospective collectors to learn more about you and your distinct narrative. In addition to purchasing artwork, collectors are increasingly investing in the history behind the artwork and the person who created the artwork. One approach to avoid marketing yourself is to send spammy connections to your CryptoArt in a personal message to friends and family. It's inefficient, and if nothing else, it will almost certainly work against you. If you're going to communicate with someone about your work, make an effort to interact with them. Make your message more personal. Additionally, repeatedly naming huge collectors or companies in your public postings is not an intelligent practice, as it will copy and paste the same message without any personalization.

9.7 Be Consistent

It's essential to keep in mind that the CryptoArt scene and NFTs, in general, are relatively new. Do not be discouraged if you are not effective right away or as rapidly as you had hoped. This is only the beginning of your journey to success. The community is warm and welcoming, and everyone is eager to assist one another in their endeavors. Continue to create, connect, and share your art with the rest of the world. Make the necessary adjustments, and don't be afraid to seek assistance when needed.

9.8 Know Worth of Your Art

How much should your artwork be sold for? Take into consideration that you will be required to pay for gas fees and minting (unless you choose to use OpenSea's gasless minting option or Cargo's Magic Minting option) when determining the price of your artworks. If you include the cost of minting and gas, you can expect to pay anywhere from $50 to $80 per piece of jewelry. As a result, your artwork would have to be significantly more expensive for you to make a reasonable profit. Additionally, if you have done next to nothing to develop your brand image, you may be fortunate enough to make a couple of selling, but your career will most likely be brief. Set a reasonable price for your artwork. Just because someone else has sold their CryptoArt for 1 ETH does not imply that you will do so as well. It takes time and works to establish your brand, which requires time and effort.

9.9 Starting with a Collection

Begin with a Collection of Items. It's a good idea to start by selling a small collection of artworks, anything from three to eight works in total. A topic and a tale should be included throughout the collection. Collectors will be motivated to purchase more than one item from you in this manner since it is always good to have the whole series.

9.10 Exhibit in Metaverses

Once you've become more familiar with the CryptoArt environment, you may begin researching the metaverses, such as Decentraland, Cryptovoxels, and Somnium Space, to further your knowledge. In these metaverses, there are virtual galleries that present art exhibitions every week. This is an excellent opportunity to promote your business while meeting new people, and it may even lead to some interview opportunities. These metaverses have a Twitter account, updated with current builds and exhibits. By following this account, you may interact with the individuals who run the galleries and arrange for a show to be held there.

There is a tremendous amount of promise in the sector, and there are several fresh and fantastic ideas being introduced daily. Remember, don't be scared to interact with others, express your individuality, and keep creating!

CHAPTER NO. 10

LIST OF 10 MOST EXPENSIVE NFTS EVER SOLD

NATHAN REAL

Chapter No. 10
List of 10 Most Expensive NFTs Ever Sold

The following will provide a list of the top ten most costly NFTs currently available on the market, as well as an explanation of why these NFTs are valued. Unique digital assets, music, photos, collectibles, GIFs, and memes are examples of non-financial-transactions (NFTs) in which the crypto civilization is willing to invest. More specifically, they have been purchasing non-fungible tokens in record numbers, resulting in the emergence of a new kind of digital assets business in recent months. Well, in only one month, and over $300 million in sales have been recorded, and the NFT markets are undoubtedly generating a substantial profit on the backs of other people's efforts. Even very young platforms are acquiring significant momentum due to the sale of these NFTs.

10.1 Every Day: The First 5000 Days

Price– $69.3 million

Although the artist formerly known as Beeple had been around for a while, he was not as well-known as you would think. The artist did sell one of the priciest NFT artworks on the market in 2021, though. "Every day: the First 5000 Days" is the title of the piece of art. Perhaps the most remarkable aspect of the transaction is that it took place inside an auction house named Christie's. After starting at $100, the bidding quickly increased in value, eventually reaching a total of $69.3 million. You could be thinking to yourself, "Wow, that's a great deal of money for some digital art." Given the technological development, isn't it apparent that we will soon be able to create digital paintings instead of actual paintings shortly? In any case, this piece of artwork was a combination of the first 5000 digital artworks created by Beeple himself. When People first began creating digital art, he didn't miss a single day of work, and he continued to do so until May 2007. As a result, many different styles, subjects, and media are included in the compilation. Even though some of the first-ever ones were not up to par, the worth of the group as a whole improved tremendously. And it is for this reason that this NFT is among the costliest NFTs ever marketed. This is without a doubt one of the most expensive non-fungible tokens in the year 2021.

10.2 CryptoPunk #3100

Price-$7.58 million

It is a new form of creation in the NFT realm, and it is called CryptoPunks. These are the very earliest NFTs to be introduced into the market. As a result of the recent explosion in the popularity of NFTs, many of them are now selling for millions of dollars! This is why CryptoPunk #3100 is also included on our list, since it is the second most costly NFT ever sold, after CryptoPunk #7804.

In truth, this CryptoPunk is among the rarest of the CryptoPunks, and it is one of the nine Aliens that make up the group of nine. Because there are only 10,000 punks available at CryptoPunks, and even more so, just nine of them are extraterrestrials. As you can see, these nine collections represent some of the most valuable they have. These coins are also ERC-20 tokens, which means they adhere to the ERC standards.

The character features blue-greenish skin in tone, and it comes with an attachment as well. The item in question is headbands, and only 406 punks have this particular accessory. Much more so since it only comes with a single attachment, which is also uncommon, and only 333 punks have a singular addition, making it even more valuable. So, this punk is unique based on the style of punk, the accessories, and the number of accessories. That is why it was sold for $7.58 million, which is a record price.

10.3 CryptoPunk #7804

Price-$7.57 million

Another CryptoPunk is included in our top ten most expensive NFTs list, this time with a $7.57 million price tag. Punk #7804 is another Alien, and this again comes with three attachments to complete the package. More specifically, the accessories include Small Shades, Cap forwards, and a Pipe, among other things. According to reports, only 254 punks are equipped with Caps Forward, 378 punks are equipped with Pipe, and 317 punks are fitted with tiny sunglasses. But, in general, the high price is due to the reality that Alien punks are tough to come by. Dylan Field was the one who brought the punk back into the organization when it initially began giving out the 10,000 CryptoPunks. In actuality, he is the founder and CEO of the technological design business Figma. But why did he spend so much money on that punk? Well, he saw the significance of this Ethereum-based NFT, which drove him to acquire it in early 2018.

10.4 Crossroads Project

Price-$6.6 million

Crossroads is another of our most costly NFTs to mention. This is another piece of artwork by Beeple, and it was sold only a few days before the enormous sale of every day took place. More importantly, the artist could sell this painting at Nifty Gateway. Also, unlike every day, this is not a collection of artwork but rather a singular piece of artwork. The object becomes even more costly as a result of the appraisal given to it in this case.

On the other hand, the painting is a political risk and a reaction to the upcoming presidential race in 2020. The artist created two copies of this, one for if Trump were to win and another for Trump to lose. This is a nice tidbit to know. In addition, the video would alter depending on the election result.

10.5 The First Tweet Generated

Price-$2.9 million

We even have the first tweet on our list of the costliest NFTs in 2021, which comes in at number two. The truth is that Twitter's CEO and creator, Jack Dorsey, sent out the first tweet after launching the service in 2006. "I'm just getting started with Twitter," the message said. And later on, he resold this tweet as a non-financial transaction (NFT) for a substantial sum of money — $2.9 million! Given the enormous reputation of the social networking site Twitter, it shouldn't come as a surprise that the first tweet would get this much interest. This is undoubtedly a novel approach to asset tokenization. In any circumstance, the originator sold this post to Oracle Chief Executive Sina Estav, who feels it is just as essential as acquiring the Mona Lisa in terms of cultural significance. The CEO went over and above by selling this tweet via the online auction site Valuables. A 5 percent cut will be taken from the marketing price in accordance with the platform's terms and conditions. Even though the post will persist on Twitter, the content has been transferred to Sina.

10.6 CryptoPunk #6965

Price-$1.54 million

Another punk appears on our list of the costliest nonferrous metals (NFTs) in 2021. As previously said, each and every Crypto-Punk has its own set of qualities and attributes that distinguish them from the others. As a result, this punk is not unusual from the others. CryptoPunk #6965 is a member of the Ape species, as seen here. It also has a Fedora as an optional attachment. More specifically, just 186 punks wear Fedoras, and there are only 24 Ape punks in the world. It is for this reason that the cost is $1.54 million! These, however, are not ERC-721 coins but are more closely related to ERC-20 tokens.

10.7 Axie Infinity Genesis Land

Price-$1.5 million

You are probably aware of how expensive certain in-game products can be for those of you who like virtual games. However, one digital game called Axie Infinity, built on the Ethereum blockchain, may have pushed it to the next level. Real-world-wise, Genesis Land is exceedingly difficult to come by in the game, and it commands a hefty price. An anonymous donor just acquired nine Genesis blocks for a staggering 1.5 million dollars. As a result, it will be one of the highest-cost nonferrous transition metals in 2021. The value has climbed significantly as the value of Ether has increased over the last several months.

10.8 CryptoPunk #4156

Price-$1.25 million

We then have CryptoPunk #4156, the costliest NFT ever traded on the market, the following item on our list. That's correct. We've got another CryptoPunk on our hands once again. A blue bandana is included with this Ape punk, which is yet another Ape punk that comes with an attachment this time around. Only 481 punks share this characteristic out of a total of 10,000 punks. And it is now owned by the Ethereum address 0xf476cd, which paid $1.25 million for it. However, purchasing CryptoPunks will necessitate the purchase of Ethereum Gas, so keep this in mind if you intend to put money in some CryptoPunks as well.

10.9 Not Forgotten, But Gone

Price—One Million Dollar

Do you want to spend millions of dollars on a revolving gummy bear video clip? This is precisely what occurred at the Nifty Gateway NFT sales department. An artist created this piece of artwork by the name of WhIsBe. According to reports, he uses a variety of gummy bears in a variety of inventive ways. More specifically, it's a 16-second movie of a revolving golden adhesive bear skeleton with the title "Not Forgotten, But Gone." This sculpture was sold for a million dollars to the artist.

10.10 Metarift

Price-$904.41 million

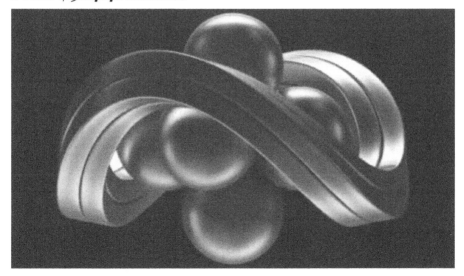

It's yet another Satoshi issue since no one understands who was the artist that created this piece of artwork. The artist is known only by the alias Pak, and no one knows who they are in real life. According to reports, Pak is well-known in the digital art community, and the mysterious nature of the piece contributed to the piece's high price of $904.41K. The NFT art consists of a number of spherical objects spinning in various directions and grouped. There are a variety of different NFT applications such as these; they are not confined to the arts!

CHAPTER NO. 11

LIST OF NFT PROJECTS TO INVEST IN 2022

NATHAN REAL

Chapter No. 11
List of NFT Projects to Invest in 2022

Our hand-picked list of the most notable NFT projects to investment for 2022 is determined based on specific criteria.

11.1 Keys to the Metaverse

This compilation of 10 K-generated art NFTs contains many fascinating features. In the beginning, they will be debuting on the top 10 blockchains. The team behind the project plans to launch 1000 each of the blockchains (BSC, Ethereum, Tron, Solana, ICP, etc.). Named 'Keys to the Metaverse,' the project gives several particularly gratifying characteristics. Each machine-produced artwork shows a KEY with an animal head on end & a collection of distinctive attributes on the other end. The project's objective is to make all the 10K distinct NFTs cross-chain. Also, the complete collection will have an open secured API layer, so any application or game may incorporate the NFTs in their project as per their inventiveness. This is one of the top NFT projects to purchase for 2022 for the following reasons:

- Each of the keys has so many varied features and properties. And if some application is merging the collections based on these features, the output may be something remarkable. Thus, raising the demand for goods swiftly.

- Since the NFTs are released across all the leading blockchains, they will harness the community existing in each chain.

- Also, because the NFTs will be cross-chain, we will witness a lot of action of the NFTs across chains shortly.

11.2 Decentraland

This is a highly renowned project with millions of people utilizing it actively. It is a virtual world entirely on the Blockchain. People get to pick their avatars and travel around freely in this Metaverse. You may purchase land within Decentraland and create whatever there. Many construct mansions, villas, exposition halls, etc., in the land they own within. The Land (parcels) you possess in DCL is an NFT. This NFT may be exchanged outside DCL on any marketplace. All the land in DCL is already taken and is growing significantly in price. Many individuals from countries like Thailand, South Korea, etc., are already preparing a life with their property. The land you own in DCL generates your money in the following ways:

- Rental money, Sale income as the property grows in value, marketing your goods, and other NFTs to the guests who come to your buildings on the site.

- DCL land pieces are selling quickly on markets like OpenSea, and it is one of the most exemplary NFT initiatives and tokens to buy for 2022.

11.3 Axie Infinity

This is a renowned blockchain game currently played by thousands across the globe. Many individuals play these games as a full-time profession to make a livelihood. Playing Axie Infinity, one may gain three categories of things. One of the game administration tokens, AXS, is already trading at $140 at the time of writing this. The firm has also just developed a facility to stake these tokens. The second piece is SLP (Smooth Love Potion), which customers buy to feed the tiny monsters. The price of SLP has also traded at $0.093 per token. The third part is the NFT collection, i.e., the Axies. These NFTs are bought and sold on NFT platforms like Open Sea. There are 283.8K listed items in OpenSea at the time of editing this page. These might be some of the most notable NFT projects to purchase and invest in 2022. Simply because these NFTs have a reason behind them, i.e., they may be used to play and earn. Also, in the future, the corporation may develop these NFTs, which will only raise the price in the coming days. Like how the Kryptokittens were trendy in 2017, the Axie infinity collectibles are for sure going to remain for long. More than simply being a work of art, these NFTs are highly dynamic, which helps them stand out from the others.

11.4 Enjin

The Enjin project seeks to offer a cross-chain blockchain network for developers to create and distribute their E2P games. The technology also makes it easier for developers to turn their in-game assets into NFTs. The Enjin currency backs the NFT's so they may be traded out in the actual world or on any market. Whenever an NFT is created here, it is injected with a set quantity of Enjin tokens, subsequently incinerated from circulation. The fascinating feature we found is the 'melting' capability, whereby the NFT owners may burn their assets at any point and receive the same value in Enjin currencies.

Enjin token might be one of the most exemplary NFT initiatives to buy for 2022 since it draws its worth from all the NFTs it backs within its platform. So, investing in this token amounts to collectively purchasing non-fungible tokens generated on the whole network.

11.5 Rouge Sharks

Rogue Sharks is a compilation of 5000 randomly generated art 3D NFTs. The crew supporting it has been on flames even before its debut. They have established a thriving community around the topic on social media, and the entire content is minted on the Solana blockchain. At the time of writing this, roughly 1500 of the total NFTs have been posted on the Solana ART market exchanged for ~60K SOL. Significantly an incredible viral expansion the project has attained. At this pace, the initiative quickly becomes like the following BASIC collections on the Solana blockchain. So, it is one of the finest NFTs to buy for 2022.

Owners of the NFT will have exclusive admittance to the 'Rouge Sharks' club. Also, they will be permitted to partake in the 'Treasure Chest' lottery.

If you are into Crypto, you may have already heard about the Shiba Inu token. It has swept the globe by storm and made numerous billionaires in a speedy period. So great is the appeal of this fantastic Meme currency. Not to forget that it's already become the 11th highest famous crypto. This extraordinary development is solely due to the beautiful society is behind. The #shibarmy is really in the thousands and is prepared to go through any wall to enhance the currency's price. The NFT collection published on OpenSea was bought out pretty rapidly, and it already has 3600+ users with a floor price of 1.18 ETH. These NFTs look extremely promising with solid community support and may fly quickly in value. It might be one of the greatest NFTs to invest in 2022.

CHAPTER NO. 12

TIPS AND TRICKS OF NFT WORLD

NATHAN REAL

Chapter No. 12
Tips and Tricks of NFT World

For non-profit organizations, it has been an exciting year. The more you spend in the space, the more you will discover that there is so much to learn. Several variables and moving elements might be challenging to keep track of. Here's a list of suggestions that are picked up along the road to assist you in getting started or if you've just begun purchasing NFTs. This is written just for beginners, and after viewing it, you will feel more confident in stepping in and getting to work purchasing and selling NFTs!

Before you begin, you should consider these:

First and foremost, this is not a 101, but if you are beginning to start, there are five different sorts of platforms that you should be familiar with. I'll include the most regularly used terms for each forum below since they'll all be critical to your success on your trip. Coinbase.com is used to purchase cryptocurrency, MetaMask Wallet stores NFTs, Opensea.io is used as a market to buy and sell NFTs, Twitter is used to communicate with other people involved in NFTs, and Discord is used for project-specific announcements and debates. Take those five steps, and you'll be ready to go!

Safety

We must discuss privacy and security now that you are prepared to purchase NFTs independently. People will work tirelessly to attempt to defraud and rob you in this environment, and you must be conscious of the dangers you are putting yourself in.

Keep these guidelines in mind:

Never click on any link and ads unless you are confident that they are legitimate.

Your Discord DMs will be bombarded with links to potentially fraudulent websites. To assist in limiting this, you may turn off direct communications from server members by visiting this page:

Beginner's Guide to NFT Techniques

- If you get responses to your Twitter postings that include links that seem to be frauds, block the individuals responsible.

- Never divulge your seed phrase to anybody! Except for you, no one else needs it, and it must be kept in a secure location.

- Avoid taking screenshots in order to decrease the possibility of your private information being shared.

- Your wallets address is visible to the public and may be shared with others. People will want your mailing address in order to send you NFTs or cryptocurrency, and it is safe to distribute this document.

- The mobile version of MetaMask is OK if you want the convenience, but be cautious not to click on any links that might lead to fraud if you use it.

- If you ever have any doubts about whether or not your account has been hacked, you may freeze your account by visiting this page:

- Make confident that you are in the correct project while using OpenSea. Fake projects that appear pretty similar to the real thing will be put up to defraud you. Also, when purchasing bundles, be specific that each NFT inside the pile is genuinely from a similar project as the rest of the heap. This is a regular fraud that you may come across.

- Consider using a tricky wallet for your high-value NFTs in order to offer an extra degree of protection.

- Hopefully, none of this has scared you away, but it's crucial to be aware of the facts, and it will all be second nature to you in no time!

The Ethereum blockchain will host the vast majority of the NFTs you will be purchasing, and each transaction will incur a cost for gas consumption. The price of gas changes regularly, and the greater the price of petrol, the more money it will cost you every transaction to complete the deal.

The second aspect to mention about gas is that the price tends to be cheaper at night and weekends when action is reduced. As a result, you should strive to make low-cost purchases throughout specific periods of the year. You wouldn't want to pay.04 ETH in gas for something that costs .01 ETH, would you?

Finally, this is a level beyond novice, but you may speed up gas if you attempt to snipe an NFT or mint a project in great demand, but this is not recommended. If you accept the additional fee, you may accomplish this by clicking on the speed up option inside a pending charge in MetaMask and then approving the transaction.

Strategy

If you can, purchase many NFTs from a single project, which permits you to sell one if you need to while still participating in the initiative.

Commons should be sold, while rares should be held. You should sell your most frequent NFTs first if you notice a program taking off and want to take some gains off the table. This is because the value increase of the uncommon NFT has an exponentially more significant trajectory if the project continues to expand.

The short idea is to look at the characteristics while searching to discover which features are more restricted. We'll cover how to detect rarity in more detail later.

Always try to maintain a tiny amount of $ETH (.1 –.2) on hand if you get a complimentary mint on your project or if a bargain of a lifetime comes up on your project. Additionally, gas is required for transactions like the listing or delisting of NFTs, making it beneficial to keep reserves on hand at all times.

Keep an eye out for selling walls. If you see 100 NFTs listed at.15, for example, know that it will take time to break through that wall and that you will likely see some undercut in the meanwhile to compensate for the delay.

Examine the purchasing activities. This will tell you how often this venture is being purchased, and the greater the number of purchases, the more optimistic the market is. This information is available for any operation in OpenSea.

CHAPTER NO. 13
FAQS

NATHAN REAL

Chapter No. 13

FAQs

What is the difference between a fungible token and a non-fungible token?

The Fungible Tokens are not distinguishable from one another and can be separated, but the Non-Fungible Tokens are distinct and inseparable. The token standards they adhere to will also vary, with the NFT adhering to ERC-721 or another comparable standard and the fungible adhering to ERC-20, respectively.

Is it possible to utilize NFTs as a kind of investment?

It is possible to employ NFTs as an investment at the moment, given the existing conditions. It is possible to acquire an NFT and sell it again for a profit. In some instances, NFT markets even enable NFT sellers to get royalties on the assets they sell. For his digital artworks, the digital artist Mike Winkelmann a.k.a. Beeple, produced a series of NFTs, which he named the Beeple series. In October of last year, he sold the first batch of NFTs, each of which was valued at $66,666.66. One of the NFTs, initially sold for $66,666.66, was recently resold for $6.6 million to a digital asset buyer in Singapore, who had initially purchased it for $66,666.66. Even while non-financial transactions (NFTs) might be regarded as an opportunity to invest, the legal issues of NFT investments have not yet been clarified in most countries. As a result, restrictions and limits on the purchase of NFTs might be anticipated depending on the investor's jurisdiction.

Is it prohibited if the NFT gives the buyer a return on their investment?

It is not unlawful as far as the NFT seller complies with the rules and regulations of the SEC or the laws and regulations of their jurisdiction. It is necessary to determine if the NFTs they are selling are assets or not. This is assessed in light of the reason for the formation and selling of the NFT. Suppose an NFT is issued in exchange for an existing non-tangible object sold as a collectible with a public guarantee of validity on the blockchain. In that case, the NFT may not be deemed a security under the Securities and Exchange Act of 1934. When NFT is issued and sold for sellers to make investment returns, the NFT is most likely to be characterized as security. Notably, minting NFT is so costly for tiny digital artists raises whether this is a problem.

Currently, the gas charge for NFTs created on the Ethereum blockchain is around $40. This is not possible in the case of low-value digital artworks. Another alternative is to mint NFTs on other less costly networks, such as Tezos or Polkadot, which are less expensive than Ethereum.

What is the best way to tell whether your NFT is genuine?

The ownership of NFTs is recorded and stored on a blockchain, and this entry serves as a digitalized pink slip in the digital world. The definition of the blockchain is a whole other bag of worms, which you can read about here.

Is the use of NFTs a novel concept?

They're becoming more popular, although they're not new. Andrew Steinwold traced the beginnings of cryptocurrencies back to blockchain-backed Colored Coins in 2012. Still, it wasn't until CryptoKitties became viral in 2017 that they were widely accepted.

Why would I want to be the proud owner of an NFT? Is it possible for me to earn money from it?

An NFT's emotional worth, comparable to actual goods (unless you're a purely utilitarian), is one of the primary reasons to get one. No one purchases lip gloss since they feel the need to do so, and they are buying it because it helps them feel when they use it. In the case of a GIF, a picture, a video, or any other digital asset, the same may be said.

The second reason is that you believe it is valuable...and that its worth will only rise in the future. You may earn money off an NFT by purchasing it at a lower price and reselling it at a higher price.

What is it about an NFT that makes it valuable?

The value of an NFT is derived from the property it signifies, which is typically something that appears to exist in the digital world, such as an authentic piece of art or a portion of digital memorabilia, and is represented by the symbol "$." It is not necessary that the NFT itself contains the digital property, but instead that it points to the location of the digital property on the blockchain. An NFT, like a concert ticket or a deed to a piece of real estate, reflects the monetary value of the thing it represents.

Do you believe that NFTs are the future of collectibles and art?

It all depends on who you speak with. Artists, athletes, musicians, celebrities, and others are drawn to NFTs because they provide a new and unique way to sell their wares — including things like memes, GIFs, and tweets — directly to their fans through social media platforms. NFTs also allow artists to program ongoing royalties if the property is sold to a new proprietor. Galleries believe they have a chance to reach a new era of collectors.

Why is NFT used in games?

Non-fungible Tokens in the gaming industry are a revolutionary concept that can significantly improve efficiency. The NFTs in-game allows the user to mint and sell the in-game investments as the NFT in NFT marketplaces, allowing the user to earn money while playing. They even paved the way for creating a single world, and NFT propels the gaming business to the next level, where players will get compensated even for participating in NFT-based games.

What is Physical NFT?

Physical NFTs are assets that are based primarily on assets that are currently available in the real world; they can be anything from a real-estate asset to any object in the real world; the digital edition of the investment will be delegated with a token that represents the physical asset, and the digital edition of the investment will be designated with a permit that means the physical commodity.

Is it possible to sell physical objects as NFT?

Yes, you may, since the physical goods that are transformed into assets will produce a digital version of themselves and include a unique identifier. Physical assets may be sold in the NFT marketplace in the same way that digital assets can be sold in the market.

What is the purpose of NFT Marketing?

The NFT environment is becoming more and more regularly filled, with multiple versions and beliefs being produced in a typical day. The marketing of NFT products and services will be an essential component of the NFT professional life. To maintain your asset's status as the center of attention in the NFT marketplace.

What is the best way to market my NFT project?

Due to their extensive knowledge and professionalism, NFT marketing companies are an excellent choice for advertising your non-profit organizations (NFOs). However, suppose you want to pursue cheap marketing. In that case, you will need to use various marketing methods, including social media marketing, influencer marketing, and other similar tactics, to keep your product in the public eye.

CONCLUSION

NATHAN REAL

Conclusion

The variety of possibilities with NFTs is almost limitless and diversified. Non-fungible tokens, in addition to serving as gaming souvenirs and work of digital art, have the potential to symbolize virtual-world property objects and even alter the game in the fashion and sports fields. More importantly, given the increasing popularity and widespread use of NFTs, it seems inevitable that platforms other than Ethereum will shift their attention away from the development of Ethereum-based NFT support in the future.

NFT is still in its early stages, but it already has great potential, and it provides artists with advantages they have never experienced before. So, it's safe to predict that more artists will be drawn to the non-fungible technology (NFT) industry in the not too away future. It is lawful for NFTs to exist outside of self-serving cryptocurrency blockchains (such as Ether) and to allow for the actual-world legal transfer of ownership of the underlying digital assets. The DIY Protocol demonstrates how non-financial transactions (NFTs) may be used to transfer genuine, legally binding ownership.

In general, NFT is a novel tool that may meet the demands of producers, consumers, and collectors of a wide range of non-digital and digital items in various contexts. As a result, they are almost certainly here to stay, or at the very least, they constitute a first stage t9oward the development of new methods for dealing with the ownership and origin of such assets. This work will accelerate recent research on NFT across a wide range of fields, including economics, computer sciences, art history, law, computational social science, and cultural evolution. Also, the findings will assist practitioners in making sense of a quickly shifting environment and inform the creation of more efficient markets and the accompanying regulatory framework.

A special gift for you!

Thank you for reading this book.

If you enjoyed it, please visit the site where you purchased it and write a brief review. Your feedback is important to me and will help other readers decide whether to read the book too.

You are very important to me, so I decided to treat you with one of my bestsellers "Option Trading Strategy" or "Blockchain 2021".

Please write me on nathanreal.books@gmail.com which of the 2 books you would like to receive for FREE.

Thank you!
—Nathan Real

Made in United States
Orlando, FL
22 January 2022

13887373R00065